COMMENDATIONS - THE BOOK

'Youth Ministry is a growing movement across the globe. In nearly every country and most major cities there are men and women who are faithful to the Gospel's call to extend the invitation to the household of God to young people. The most pressing issue for most of them is straightforward, practical and culturally sensitive resources to guide their ministry. To serve this need, my friend and long time youth ministry leader Fraser Keay and global friends have created just such a resource. Carefully avoiding context-specific pragmatic structures, Youth Ministry Across the Continents provides the heart and soul of youth ministry as expressed around the world. This is a great tool no matter where you serve, and it will be with you for years to come."

- Chap Clark, PhD, Professor of Youth, Family and Culture; Fuller Theological Seminary, U.S.A.

Author of *Hurt 2.0: Inside the World of Today's Teenagers* and *Sticky Faith: Everyday Ideas to Build Lasting Faith in Your Kids*

"This is a book I wish I'd had 35 years or so ago when I began in youth ministry! There's nothing better than learning from practitioners with a thought-through and a prayed-through approach to ministry, and this book is full of such people. If you are a youth minister you will keep coming back to this book for wisdom and insight."

- Rev. Nigel James, City Temple Elim Church, Cardiff, Wales; Tour Pastor, Third Day

"This is a creative, provocative and educational book by Spirit-filled and vision-oriented young leaders from diverse cultural backgrounds. It will definitely be beneficial for young church workers across the globe as a source of encouragement and empowerment."

- Rev. Prof. Frederick John, Vice Principal, St Thomas Theological College, Karachi, Pakistan

"Reading Youth Ministry Across the Continents left me thankful for the great variety of people who dedicate themselves to sharing Jesus with young people across the world. It is a fabulous resource by youth ministry practitioners for youth ministry practitioners."

- **Rev. Graham Stanton, Lecturer in Practical Theology, Ridley College, Melbourne, Australia**

Youth Ministry Across The Continents is an excellent book for anyone who believes that youth are the future of the nations. The book is inspiring and exciting, but still very practical. Authors from different cultural backgrounds share key principles and best practice for working with youth. I myself, as a mother, got support and inspiration from this book, so I warmly recommend it!"

- **Sari Essayah, Member of Parliament and President of the Finnish Christian Democrats, Helsinki, Finland**

"This book is an answer to prayer. For youth ministers, it gives a good dose of inspiration and encouragement as you read about the life journeys, struggles and victories of others to whom God has given the same burden and passion for youth. This is a God-breathed gift to those in youth ministry. This book is definitely a 'must-read' for every pastor, leader or volunteer with a heart to serve God by reaching young people."

- **Pastor Rommel 'Ru' De La Torre, His Life City Church, Pampanga and Laguna, The Philippines and Los Angeles, U.S.A.**

"This book, which records the 'I-BARE-my-heart' stories of top-notch youth workers across the world, will lead to 'I-now-DARE-to-attempt-this' decisions in your youth ministry."

- **Dr. Duke Jeyaraj, Founder & Evangelist, Grabbing the Google Generation from Gehenna Mission, Hyderabad, India**

"A great guide to balanced youth ministry, a must-read book for every committed youth worker, parents and pastors. The book will surely assist any focused youth minister in planning and executing for success.

YMAC is not just another book on theory, but is about proven principles and examples that will work cross-culturally."

- **Williams Burga Likka, Senior Pastor, Evangelical Church Winning All (ECWA) Church, Yaba, Lagos, Nigeria**

"The unique cocktail of international and multicultural testimonies about youth ministry make this book a must-read. It's authentic and will make you wise as you grow as a leader and discipler of young people. This is good stuff!"

- **Martin Koornstra, Leider Royal Mission, Royal Mission Leader, The Netherlands**

COMMENDATIONS - THE AUTHORS

Ron Irving from Australia

"I have known Ron for over 20 years. He and I started Bible college together, when we were both much younger. From the early days of engaging with Ron, his passion for youth and Jesus were very evident. His desire to see as many young people experience the transforming power of Jesus was contagious. In the last decade, I have had the honour of being his Senior Minister. What has always stood out to me is the size of Ron's heart for others, especially the next generation.

His continued passion and wisdom as a seasoned leader continues to impact others in such a way that more and more young people are either directly challenged by his ministry or released themselves to be kingdom influencers.

I have no doubt that Ron will continue to powerfully engage the next generation to be culture shapers for the kingdom of God."

- Ian Barnett, Senior Minister, Figtree Anglican Church, Wollongong, NSW, Australia

Nathan Chiroma from Nigeria

"I have known Nathan for over forty years now. He loves God and he is very passionate about youth ministry; to him it is second nature. He loves young people and has influenced many in Nigeria who are now active youth pastors in various churches. I have watched him very closely and I have found him to be a man with a high level of integrity. I consider him to be a great asset for the church universal, and in Africa in particular. I have full confidence in his calling as a believer, a teacher, a pastor and a counsellor."

- Rev. Dr. Barje Maigadi, Senior Pastor of ECWA Wuse II, Abuja, Nigeria

Anne De Jesus-Ardina from The Philippines

"I have for many years been a witness to the strategic ministry of Anne Ardina towards the youth in the churches and in the community. She is the Program Director and Professor of the youth ministry program of Alliance Graduate School in Manila, the Philippines. As such, she equips prospective youth pastors who in turn will train leaders in the churches and reach out to the youth in the community. She is not only an academic but also conducts training seminars for youth leaders in the churches and in youth conferences. She writes and edits discipleship and leadership training materials for youth work. She has served as adviser to the Pastors' Kids fellowship in our denomination. Her ministry, therefore, of training youth leaders and pastors has far reaching effects."

- Dr. Rodrigo Tano, Bishop, Christian and Missionary Alliance Churches of the Philippines

Fraser Keay from Scotland

"Fraser is a man utterly devoted to the Lord Jesus Christ. His years of work with youth brought vitality, passion, and godly purpose to American teens saturated with comfort and the pleasures of the world. Fraser desires to see God's chosen leaders of all ages follow their call with grace, integrity, and passion - the very way he leads his own life. Knowing him up close, and seeing him in front of others for almost 15 years, there is a clear consistency between these two worlds. Refreshing and needed! Great depth without being stuffy, accessible without being shallow, I am sure this book will bring biblical insights for leaders of all ages and stages of youth ministry."

- Mark, Pastor, The Way Church, Denver, U.S.A.

Younus Samuel from India

"At New Life, Younus has been the driving force for the growth of our Youth Alive services which have gone from 60 to 600 young people each week. His love for the Lord and his passion to reach out to the youth through creative media arts has made it a great place to 'hang out'. His enthusiasm and energy pull in young people to try out the delightful way of walking and enjoying a new life with Jesus Christ!"

- Rev. Arlene Stubbs, Senior Pastor, New Life Assembly of God Church, Secunderabad, Hyderabad, India

Matt Gregor from Wales

"I had the privilege of working alongside Matt for 13 years and saw how he took a small, struggling youth group and transformed it over time into a thriving, life-giving community of young people. As well as having a massive heart to reach young people and young adults with the Gospel, Matt is equally enthusiastic about training and equipping the next generation of youth leaders. Many of these new leaders are teenagers themselves. What Matt shares comes from the coal-face of weekly youth ministry in a city centre church, and will strengthen and encourage you in the task of winning young people to Jesus. May the Lord bless you as you read."

- Steve Ball, Senior Pastor, City Temple Church, Cardiff, Wales

Zeeshan James from Pakistan

"I have known Zeeshan for over six years now. He loves the Lord and is very enthusiastic about working with youth in Pakistan. He has been working with IMPACT-PAKISTAN for many years and I appreciate his ministry. He really has a heart and burden for young people, which is why he travels all over Pakistan to train and equip the youth leaders of Pakistan. I have trust in him and he is a great asset to our church."

- Rt. Rev. Ernest Jacob, Bishop of Anglican Orthodox Church in Pakistan

Eero Haarala from Finland

"I have known Eero for about 7-8 years through the gatherings of Finnish Pentecostal Youth Pastors and other different nationwide events. We have been ministry colleagues since September 2014 when I became the Senior Pastor at the church where he serves. Eero has been a dedicated long-term, youth pastor for over 14 years and has done a lot of good for the youth ministry of Finnish Pentecostal churches nationwide. He has a good understanding of the whole landscape. He now serves as the Chairman of the National Board of Youth Ministries of the Pentecostal Churches of Finland and is also a member of the board of the Pentecostal Church of Finland. His is quick-witted and expresses his opinions well!"

- Matti Niemelä, Senior Pastor, Pentecostal Church of Joensuu, Finland

Gary McCusker from the USA

"It is not an overstatement to call Gary McCusker a minor legend in the community here. Gary's dedication to the young men and women of our town started almost twenty years ago in the wake of the Columbine High School shootings of 1999. Gary heard God's call to give his life to student ministry and has never looked back. Under his direction, the student ministry of Parker Evangelical Presbyterian Church became a model for the other churches in our town, and the relationships Gary built continue to this day. Each year he is called on to perform weddings and baptize the children of the students he grew to love so much. Though his job description has shifted, he continues to serve as the freshman baseball coach at Ponderosa High School which allows him to continue to impact the lives of so many of our young people. Literally hundreds serve and follow Jesus all over the world because of the man they still affectionately call 'GMac'."

- Doug Resler, Senior Pastor, Parker Evangelical Presbyterian Church, Parker, Colorado, USA

Lorna McIntosh from Scotland

"Lorna is an outstanding youth worker and an inspiring follower of Jesus Christ. At St John's Church in Linlithgow, where we were church leaders together, I had the joy of baptising many young people as a result of Lorna's relational skills in leadership, discipleship and one-to-one mentoring. Her ministry stretches beyond local church. She cares passionately about the wider church in Scotland, teaching & inspiring young people throughout the nation with Scripture Union, Alpha, and others. She also has a great heart for the worldwide church. Lorna regularly leads teams of young people and adults to serve the church in Rwanda, Burundi & Romania, and in partnership with Open Doors UK travels extensively to minister to the persecuted church around the world. I count it a privilege to call myself one of Lorna McIntosh's co-workers in the Gospel."

- Glen Cormack, Pastor, New Life Baptist Church, Northallerton, England

Mark Stoorvogel from Holland

"I have had the privilege of ministering alongside Mark for 5 years now. I am amazed to see how God has used Mark in a mighty way to touch teenagers and young people in our city, and way beyond, with His love. As a youth pastor Mark has been focusing on building a kingdom culture community of teenagers and young people that passionately love God and seek to know Him more intimately. And that is exactly what I see happen: a young generation hungry and thirsty for God and more of Him. I believe that Mark has been instrumental in this. The reason I see is this: Mark understands his first calling not as reaching young people with the gospel, although that is infinitely important; Mark feels called foremost to be a passionate lover of Jesus himself in all that He is and all that He does. And that is what gets teenagers and young people fired up for Jesus."

- Theo van den Heuvel, Senior Pastor, Stadskerk | VBG, Free Baptist Church of Groningen, The Netherlands

YOUTH MINISTRY ACROSS THE CONTINENTS

ELEVEN YOUTH PASTORS FROM TEN COUNTRIES ON THE KEY BUILDING BLOCKS FOR EFFECTIVE YOUTH WORK LEADERSHIP IN THE LOCAL CHURCH

EDITOR AND CONTRIBUTOR

FRASER KEAY

PUBLISHED BY FIRST HALF LEADERSHIP

British Library Cataloguing in Publication Data

A catalogue record for this book is available from the British Library

ISBN 978-0-9954729-0-7

The publisher's aim is to help develop emerging leaders by producing high quality books that serve those of faith or none.

www.firsthalfleadership.com

DEDICATION

For Anna, my greatest encourager and critic, the combination of whose beauty and intelligence is, in my opinion, unmatched.

TABLE OF CONTENTS

Each contributor has their own chapter in which they introduce themselves then cover the same core youth ministry topics. Some have contributed to two additional chapters, 'Some Advice when Looking at a Youth Ministry Role' and 'If You are Thinking of Leaving Front-line Ministry'.

FOREWORD

It was early 2014 when a guy I didn't know began emailing with an idea. He found out I was a presenter at Youthwork Summit 2014 in Manchester, UK, and he insisted that we meet. I respect drive and passion... he had an idea for a book...so I agreed to listen. So, in the midst of hundreds of youth workers chatting away during a break, Fraser shared with me the vision for this book.

I love Youth Ministry Across the Continents because of its premise... experienced youth workers on every continent sharing their stories, for better or worse. I love YMAC because of its pattern....each author addressing the same aspects of ministry. I love YMAC because of its potential...for actual learning ourselves. It is so helpful to look over the shoulders of others to see/hear how they do what they do. I had several "I never thought of that" moments as I read along.

This book is a treasure, so enjoy the journey as you absorb the passion, setbacks and wisdom of these wonderful youth workers!

Len Kageler, Ph.D., Department Chair, Youth & Family Studies, Nyack College, NYC, U.S.A.

Author of Youth Ministry in a Multifaith Society (InterVarsity Press, 2014) and *Don't Do This....Learning From the Screw Ups Of Youth Ministry Leaders* (Youth Cartel, 2016).

ABOUT THE EDITOR, FRASER KEAY

As well as working in the public sector, Fraser has served on three church staff teams in three countries. He has spent many years successfully recruiting, developing and encouraging younger leaders. His books are designed to motivate, support and educate those who are in their first half of life and leadership. For more information please see the website www.firsthalfleadership.com

Fraser is married with two grown up children and lives in Glasgow, Scotland. He holds a B.A. (Hons) Public Administration and a Master's Degree in Divinity from Denver Theological Seminary, Colorado, U.S.A.

For brief videos introducing each of the contributors please go to the website www.firsthalfleadership.com.

INTRODUCTION

Some years ago, I had it in mind to write a different kind of youth ministry book. There are many good books out there, but I wanted something written by current and recent youth pastors from a variety of countries who can share a range of perspectives on local church youth ministry. That way, readers like you can get some help and encouragement from a number of long-term youth pastors - from ten countries across the globe - on how to build a solid, local church youth ministry.

Each of the eleven contributors has at least ten years' part or full time youth ministry experience; most have many, many more. They all write on eleven topics including how they began in youth ministry, how to look after your own soul and how to lead a team well. The full list is below. Some have contributed to two chapters at the end with some thoughts on what you should consider if moving to a new youth pastor role, and things to reflect on if you are thinking about leaving youth ministry. You will be able to compare and contrast their advice on the same youth ministry topics and, in doing so, will learn about differences and similarities. Some of the differences in approach and style reflect personality and some reflect culture. Others are to do with the church the writer belongs to, be it Presbyterian, Pentecostal, Anglican, Baptist, Independent Evangelical, Assemblies of God, or Christian and Missionary Alliance Churches.

This brings a certain richness to the book and encourages us to think more broadly. You will resonate more with some than others depending on your personality or the ministry situation in which you currently find yourself. Most importantly, each person writes from the 'coalface' - from practice and not just theory; from experiences of joy and of sadness; from defeat as well as victory. They are humans who know that they need the power of God to minister to young people and who readily testify to God's grace and goodness.

This book is ideal to pick up and read a chapter at a time; or you could review what each contributor has to say on a certain topic. It is recommended for people at all stages of youth ministry - whether in training or further down the line. It is accompanied by the website www.firsthalfleadership.com on which you can find more details about, and videos by, each of the contributors. The website also brings the contributors together in a 'virtual' sense since we have never all met together in person despite this book drawing us into a joint task. Many of the writers do not speak English as their first language; I decided to leave it to each writer whether to use American or British grammar and spelling.

If you are looking for some more information on the countries represented in this book, I would recommend 'Operation World', which is a superb resource for statistics and information on every nation, as well as a prayer guide, see www.operationworld.org. If you come from a nation not represented by any of the authors, have at least ten years' part or full time local church youth ministry experience, and would like to be considered as an additional author in the future, then please contact me via the website.

Reader, you have in your hands over 160 years' worth of international youth work experience gained in the last three decades by many still doing youth ministry. May you be blessed as you read it. I know I have been in bringing it all together.

Fraser Keay, Scotland
www.firsthalfleadership.com
@firsthalfleader

I. FOUNDATIONS

1. My background and how I got into youth ministry

2. Looking after your own soul

3. Singleness, marriage & children

4. Organising yourself and your ministry

II. YOUNG PEOPLE

5. Keeping your evangelism edge sharp

6. Communicating with youth

7. Pastoral care of young people

III. OTHER PEOPLE

8. Working with schools

9. Leading a team and developing others

10. Parents

11. You and senior church leaders

Chapter 1
Ron Irving from Australia

With a heart of gratitude to our triune God, this chapter is dedicated to my wife Julie, and children Jacob and Emily, whose love and support is a constant symbol and tangible expression of God's grace and kindness. Further, it is dedicated to the communities cf St Johns Park Anglican, Ulladulla Anglican and Figtree Anglican Churches whom have kindly allowed me to develop these ideas through, often flawed praxis of youth ministry.

1. My background and how I got into youth ministry

I grew up in the western suburbs of the city of Sydney - the working class suburban part, not the spectacular harbour and beaches part - and spent the first thirty years of my life wondering how to escape the city. It's not that it was all bad, but regular holidays around rural parts of Australia stirred a desire to be more connected with the Australian bush (the rural part).

My family attended a local Anglican Church, which was strong on preaching and Bible teaching. While I am increasingly grateful for this, at the time it gave me more of a sense of God's transcendence than his immanence, and so it left me with an impersonal and disinterested God rather than an intimate and loving one. It did not really help me enough as a teenager, with my own struggles for identity and significance.

I wasn't sure what I wanted to do when I left school, so I went ahead and got a job. It was there that God showed me his intimate concern for people through a colleague's faithful life and witness. After many discussions, much prayer (from a range of people) and a little too much to drink one farewell lunchtime, I felt like I was in a pit - desperate to feel loved. My colleague told me "You know what you need to do, just do it". He meant that I needed to stop resisting Jesus and let him rule my life. It was then that whatever faith I had became personal and real for me, and I allowed Jesus to direct the course of my life.

I was surprised, and a little offended, by God's call into youth ministry a year later; it came through someone I hardly knew at a youth leadership training conference. My passion then, and now, was that the local church

would provide healthy and helpful environments where the timeless reality of God's grace and truth in Jesus could be connected with the contemporary world of young people.

After theological and ministry training I started local church youth
ministry full time in 1994, in the very multi-cultural and working class
south west of Sydney. In the same year I was married and also had two
major operations resulting in the removal of my left lung - a miraculous
series of events that allowed early diagnosis and intervention, and has
prolonged my earthly life by any measure. I served there for six years
and had two children before God allowed me to go to a rural town on
the New South Wales South Coast - not quite the bush, but definitely
not the city! The combination of youth ministry in church and school
environments in both suburban and rural settings led to the next ministry move in January 2005 to Wollongong, NSW. With a population of
205,000 some call it a city, but to me it's just a big country town (about
1.5 hrs south of Sydney). My role there at Figtree Anglican Church has
changed over the ten years but currently has me overseeing ministry to
children, youth and young adults (aged 0-30 or so), with the emphasis on
developing young leaders.

I am a contributing author to the Australian publication 'Youth Ministry on the Front Foot', and am also slowly writing my own work that
will reflect on the theology and practice of healthy Christian culture in
the local church.

2. Looking after your own soul

One of the things you realise after a few years of full time ministry is
that not everyone makes it. Just like in running races, people get going
quickly but soon they are losing steam or dropping out of the race.

Actually, the running analogy works quite well when I think about
looking after yourself. The secret to running a long way, to not tiring
out or dropping out (either literally or metaphorically) is in managing
the heart rate properly. Running up a hill will push up the heart rate and
needs to be met with a recovery time to maintain the run. The downhill
runs are great ways to be refreshed, to let the gravity do the work and let
the heart recover.

In addition to - and as an expression of nurturing my personal relationship with Jesus through Bible reading, prayer and life in Chris-

tian community - I have found exercise, family and friends to be a great source of re-energising my soul.

Exercise

I run. Hence the running analogy. I run three or four times a week. When I exercise regularly my brain and body work better. I think more clearly. I deal with discouragement better. I have a greater ability and desire to be present with people. But mostly I remember my humanity and who I am before the Lord God. When I run, I allow myself to be human, to be who God has made me to be and to remember that life is more than ministry. When I run, I look to the mountains (I don't run up them though) and the lake and the sky. I listen to the birds. I greet people with a friendly, if not too puffed, "Hi" and I thank God for who He is. I am reminded that He is the Mighty and Powerful Lord God, Creator, Sustainer and Ruler of all. My body is exhausted but my soul is refreshed.

Family

When you are in any leadership role in a church the whole family is on display, and if details that are otherwise personal become public it can easily bring bitterness and resentment. And bitterness does bad things to your soul. So part of looking after my soul has been trying to look after my family. One little thing that we have done is to live 10 minutes' drive from the church. It's far enough for me to switch off on the way home, close enough to be involved in community life. I've often used the drive to or from the office to mentally change gears by going from husband and dad to pastor... or back again. As small as it is, it has helped treasure this part of my life and guard my heart from bitterness in ministry. Sometimes bitterness still creeps in, which is where I have found good friends to be really important!

Friends

Get some good friends around you, commit to each other, and stick with them. I regularly spend time with a couple of guys that I've known for twenty years - my whole time in ministry. We share life together. We know each other well. We have lived through each other's highs and lows. We have prayed, counselled and cared. We remind each other of the things that matter most, and help each other see things we can be blinded to. They help me persevere in ministry but, more importantly, they help me persevere with Jesus. I trust I help them also.

3. Singleness, Marriage and Family

I married at the age of 24, eight weeks after finishing my studies at Bible College, and 2 weeks before commencing my first full time ministry position. The main thing I've learnt (actually still learning) is to listen to your wife, even when you may not like what she says. Your wife knows you well, wants the best for you personally and wants your ministry to flourish. I'm glad my wife has had the confidence to speak clearly into our marriage and my ministry. It has been good, though not always easy, for me and the ministry.

We have found that we need to work hard to ensure that we have time together. At first, this felt a little unromantic and lacking in spontaneity. However, it has been important to have structures within our marriage so that it can thrive amidst the relational demands of pastoral ministry. Four things strike me as significant as I reflect on marriage, family and ministry.

First, make time to connect

The moment when we are both first home in the afternoon/evening we will sit down and have a coffee and chat. We made that decision early on in ministry and I know it has helped us connect in times when we may have naturally disconnected.

Secondly, we have protected family time

That time between 5pm and 7pm is crucial for family life. We have worked hard to keep it free, allowing our family to have dinner together most nights and for my involvement in the 'bath and bedtime' routines when our children were younger.

Thirdly, we've maintained regular days off and annual holidays

I know all the reasons why this can be hard... but you really need to just do it. Strike out the days in your diary, don't take work related calls, don't check your email, stay off social media.

Fourthly, celebrate your wedding anniversary and commit some financial resources to it

A mentor of mine told me that it's the one time of the year when you can go wild on the credit card. He was exaggerating, yet making a point. Invest in your marriage - it's incredibly valuable.

The pressures that come upon a marriage can be quite intense. As a pastor you invest a lot of time caring for others. You need to make sure you care for your wife and family. I see this is an important part of living a kingdom-orientated life as a follower of Jesus. Loving my family is an expression of love for God, and of his fatherly love for me.

My children are now 20 and 18. They have grown up through our church's youth ministry and have been blessed by having wonderful young leaders who have loved and nurtured them. For me, their high school years have been a great learning experience as I have seen youth ministry first hand through the eyes of a parent. Embrace these opportunities. If you stay in youth ministry for a long time and have teenage children, work out how to allow them to have space and identity apart from you in the ministry and at the same time enjoy the incredible gift that God has given you in them.

During the last year, my eldest child has been a leader in our youth ministry. Now I am learning to listen to my children's ideas on youth leadership and ministry. Another challenge. Another joy.

4. Organising yourself and your ministry

Your ability to be organised is directly proportional to your ability to be able to empower people and build teams in ministry. I know a few freaks who have the natural ability to be organised. Most of us, though, are so keen to get into *doing* the ministry that we neglect to *organise* the ministry. But neglecting to organise the ministry negatively affects the amount of ministry that gets done.

I naturally leave details to the last minute. I also have a fairly large sense of personal responsibility. Early in ministry this meant I'd be stressing out before a program or event as I ran around doing all sorts of things that others would have been happy to do had I been organised and asked. I have learnt to be organised by spending time planning before I get into the doing. Whether this is through a list, a detailed diary or a Gantt chart isn't the most important issue, just finding a way to be organised is! So, find a way to be organised. Find some organised people around you and ask them to help you. Plan in advance, perhaps a term (semester) ahead, then a year ahead... and for those who are entering full time ministry work, plan five years ahead.

A few years ago, I enrolled in a diploma of management course to build my organisation skills when it comes to people, tasks and events. This was incredibly beneficial for my ministry development. If you are just starting out in ministry, whether as a volunteer or in some paid capacity, work hard to get at least a term ahead of yourself. Planning a term ahead will help you know the leadership resources you need so you can empower people to take on roles. This will build teams that will both help your ministry grow and enable you to do ministry without being isolated. Once you've got a term in front, spend some time thinking about your longer term plans and goals. Write them down. Plan how you are going to achieve them. Find someone who will keep you accountable for them.

Furthermore, work out how to deal with detail. Some have an eye for detail. Others don't. Know how detailed you are, and get others around you that will help you manage your weaknesses. Ministry is best done in teams because no single believer is the body. We are the body together. Some are great dreamers and visionaries. Others are good at the detail. Do whatever you can to get people around you who will help you be organised.

I use an electronic diary and set reminders to assist me in being organised. I put all meetings in my diary, but I also put some work projects into my diary. Planning the time to plan, creating a timeslot in your diary is the first step to getting it done. Of course, you need to treat that appointment with the same respect as any other appointment! Keep it, and reap the benefits that being organised brings to ministry.

5. Keeping your evangelism edge sharp

Personal evangelism was never easy for me. I wanted it to be different but struggled for many years. While I'm still no evangelist I have learnt some things over time that have helped me personally, as well as the ministry I lead. Reflecting on my youth years, I realised I lacked three things as I sought to evangelize: confidence in God; trust in the work and power of the Holy Spirit; and an ability to share his gospel and my faith. So rather than adopt a guilt-driven approach, which doesn't work anyway, in our ministry we endeavour to equip young people in those three areas.

Confidence in God

Evangelism is never disconnected from discipleship. Growing disciples learn to see God in his grandeur, able to overcome the biggest of our obstacles. They learn the reality of passages like Isaiah 40 and trust God as all powerful. Further, they grow in the confidence that Paul has in Romans 1 where he speaks of being unashamed of the gospel because it is the power of God. Confidence in God is the first building block to youth evangelism.

Trusting in the power and work of the Holy Spirit

Young people have an incredible mission field two hundred or so days of the year at their school. In the first year of high school, we spend time encouraging our Christian youth to live good lives of love amongst their friends and to pray for the Spirit of God to work in their friends. This is not to give them a way out of evangelism, but the right way in. God is already working in the hearts and lives of people around us and he wants us to speak to them in trusting partnership with him.

Able to share the gospel and faith

Equipping youth so that they are confident in sharing faith is no easy feat. Over the years I have used a variety of tools and programs but have seen none work more effectively than XEE (Evangelism Explosion). We stage the learning of XEE throughout the school years. By the end of Year 10 (at the age of 15) our young people have the ability to share the gospel and lead people to faith. Practical experience is vital in this learning. To this end, leaders continually encourage youth and talk with them about their joys and challenges in evangelism, reminding them of God's power and the Spirit's work when things are tough. The current Australian culture is very hard ground for evangelism.

We also give youth from Year 10 up an opportunity to evangelise and train others in evangelism through a short term mission that we run each July. We take them to partner with other churches and train and equip other Christians to share faith. This experience, particularly because it is cross-cultural, helps their vision of God expand, their confidence in the work of the Holy Spirit to grow, and their awareness of their ability to share faith to sky-rocket.

I have noticed how, when mission drifts from the heart of the local youth ministry, the local youth ministry has really lost its heart. Keeping our evangelism sharp keeps the whole youth ministry sharp!

6. Communicating with youth

To determine what to teach young people, I first start with the question, "What do we want a disciple of Jesus who has grown up in this ministry to look like?". In the 6 years of High School Ministry it is impossible to teach absolutely everything you would want a disciple to know (even if 'youth' ministry is expanded a bit beyond that to a 10 year time-frame). Realising that allows you to step back and start with what we want these disciples to look like when they are 18 or 20. A goal is then established to determine what to teach and preach.

Our next step is to ask, "To whom are we teaching/preaching?". This further guides our decision making and ensures we keep engaging with young people in their ever changing world. There are four distinct groups whom we have an opportunity to teach within youth ministry:

1. those not very interested in Jesus;
2. those who would not confess to be believers but who are interested in finding out about Jesus;
3. those who are believers; and
4. those who are self-starters and want to teach themselves.

Rather than teaching doctrine classes to the disinterested (Group 1) we save that systematic style of teaching for the self-starters (Group 4). Teaching for those who are disinterested (Group 1) or who are checking things out (Group 2) is more focused on discovering who Jesus is. It's the milk and solids principle that Paul speaks of in 1 Corinthians 3:2. As a parent, I remember the slow introduction of solids into the diet of my children. It is perplexing when teaching and preaching is done in a manner that seems like feeding meat to babies!

Our core small group ministry for youth has a curriculum map that ensures a mix of practical skills (e.g. how to be a good friend or how to share the gospel) with some study of books in the Bible. There is quite a bit of meat in the diet because we are aiming to teach Groups 3 and 4, but the diet is broader than meat to ensure not just balance but nutrition and life. Our teaching program for Groups 1 and 2 is much more centred on the stories and teaching of Jesus found in the Gospels.

In a similar way, different *styles* of teaching better suit different groups. Expository teaching with a strong focus on bringing the key idea or 'big idea' of the passage to life in practical and useful ways is the preferred method of preaching within the youth ministry I oversee. Whilst we collaborate with leaders and youth about ideas for teaching and preaching programs, the decisions regarding what is being taught are generally made by team leaders and ministry staff.

At the end of the day, the key to effective communication is how we engage with young people. We see higher levels of involvement where young people are more engaged. Discussion groups, question and answer sessions, as well as summer and weekend camps seem to be the most effective learning strategies and environments. When the young people are away together the teaching is focused and quite intense; however, the community culture, sense of focus, and the availability of time to think things through and ask questions in a loving environment, seems to assist in the effectiveness of teaching and preaching.

7. Pastoral care of young people

Pastoral care is essential to the ongoing health and vitality of youth ministry. But it's not the glamorous side of youth ministry. It's not what people see or even seek to emulate. It's not particularly cool and it doesn't give any 'quick-wins' that church leaders or parents may pat you on the back for. In fact, it often goes unnoticed. But if it's not there, very quickly the whole ministry can start to be impacted.

Reactive pastoral care

Often pastoral care is *reactive*. By reactive, I simply mean pastoral care that reacts to someone or something. We offer reactive pastoral care when people are sick, when there's an unexpected tragedy, when world events give rise to some extra reflection. This pastoral care should involve practical and spiritual aspects. Perhaps a hospital visit involves playing a game and then reading Scripture together. Sometimes after unexpected tragedies we have just created a space for people to come and be together and pray together. There's nothing wrong, and much right, about reactive pastoral care. But good youth ministry will also develop *proactive* systems of pastoral care.

Proactive pastoral care

This will provide a robustness and health to a ministry that enables you to be prepared for the unexpected. Proactive pastoral care with young people may be helping them understand things about life that they haven't yet experienced so they can be more prepared to deal with them. Jesus talked with his disciples about his coming death and resurrection on a few occasions. They didn't fully understand, but it did help prepare them for what was coming. In a similar way we know the transition to high school, or out of high school, comes with its own challenges. To be preparing them for these challenges by talking with young people, and helping them make decisions based on their faith relationship with Jesus, is to be involved in proactive pastoral care. Without being morbid, it's good to take opportunities to talk about death with young people as well. It helps prepare them for their first personal experiences of someone close to them dying. The pressures applied to youth during the final year of school is another opportunity for pastoral care. Spend time talking with them about what is coming up. Provide additional support, for example through prayer breakfasts, so you are there with them - caring before things explode.

By combining both reactive and proactive pastoral care we help ensure the complete person is being looked after or "pastored". It is about holistic support and growth.

Parents and safety

All pastoral care with young people needs to honour the parental relationship and promote the safety of the young person. It's easy to mix up your own emotional needs in the caring of young people. This can be incredibly damaging. Maintain transparency and ensure there are people around who can give you the personal support you need.

Systems

Systems of pastoral care are very helpful, especially if you are leading a ministry of more than 8-10 people. At that size you can't do it by yourself. We have small group networks that provide pastoral care for young people. However, this creates the need to care pastorally for those leaders who lead these groups. So, we also have a coaching system that seeks to support leaders by helping them be focused, resourced and spiritually sustained. As a ministry grows, it becomes the job of the leader to provide pastoral care for leaders who will in turn provide it for young people.

8. Working with schools

If 'battle' is an analogy for youth ministry leadership (and let's face it, sometimes it feels like that), ministry in schools is the front line. Adrenaline flows, soldiers are under fire, weapons are revealed, truces are welcome relief, victories are sweet, white flags are raised, and going home is a hope that sometimes seems too distant.

In Australia, each state has slightly different practices regarding working in schools. The state in which I live and minister (New South Wales - NSW) has legislation that permits authorised religious groups to teach Special Religious Education to students of that nominated religion for up to one hour per week across the school year. This is done in negotiation with the school itself. It's a pretty incredible opportunity!

'Scripture Teachers' - volunteers from local churches who take these classes once a week are able to teach our 'religious data' (i.e. the Bible) according to our tradition's interpretation. For me that is Christian, Evangelical, and Anglican. The aim is for children to understand what faith is and become associated with a faith community, i.e. the church. We are able to teach in high schools as well, but finding volunteers is much harder.

Scripture Teaching is a vital component of effective youth ministry in schools in NSW. I would suggest its alternatives, i.e. *any* work with schools wherever you live, are just as vital. Here's why:

1. In NSW it's an opportunity to proclaim the gospel in the context of a developing teacher/student relationship.
2. It provides a bridge through the relationship with a faith community, like a youth group.
3. It keeps you sharp in your thinking and practice regarding adolescent culture and contemporary apologetics.
4. It provides links into a school community which increase opportunities for service or other pastoral ministry.
5. It encourages and supports the Christian high school students who front up every day, trying to live for Jesus amongst their friends in the school.

Establishing effective ministry in high schools is hard work, but the opportunity is too great to neglect. I have taught 4 x 45 minute periods back-to-back on a Friday morning at a high school in South West Sydney where gangs dropped in on a regular basis... not to play handball! Many Friday afternoons were spent in my own sort of recovery session, re-energising for the evening ahead. It was exhausting and often despairing. But over the years it had a valuable impact on myself, students and staff.

Effective ministry in schools happens when we take whatever relational opportunities are available. I coached a rugby team at a school where I also taught Scripture. The mutual respect, enjoyment and life-sharing that came in the coaching context was incredible.

The youth community at my church has also had days where we have served local schools. On one occasion, we painted a special needs room and organised for a bike path to be built in an area for students with special needs. We also did some general tidying up. It was great for our youth community and for the school, which put a huge message of thanks to the church on their front notice board. It wasn't what we were seeking, nor the reason to do it, but it did show how they had been touched by Jesus' love as kingdom life was enacted for them.

9. Leading a team and developing others

Jesus led a team of young leaders. Twelve of them. They had all sorts of experiences and expectations. They had different personalities, gifting and passions. Jesus led several of them to become world changers. Yet others fade into the pages of history quite quickly after his departure. And one of them totally undermined the cause Jesus was leading them in for personal gain, causing huge trauma for the team. We can learn a lot, and be liberated a lot, as we think about how Jesus led that team.

Understand people

Different people have different needs. The group of people described above presented a variety of challenges and strengths that Jesus had to manage. Any team will be made up of a variety of people. Some you will naturally get along with more easily than others. Leading and developing a team will mean looking for the strengths that different people bring to the team and helping to maximise those strengths for the good of the team and its purposes, even when they drive you to despair.

Do yourself out of a job

Jesus did. He had to. He knew his tenure was short. About 3 years. (Incidentally, about the same as the average youth pastor here in Australia). Jesus actively looked for opportunities to help his young leaders grow and take on new responsibilities. Sometimes they messed it up and he had to fix it up (see Luke 9:37-43), but these were valuable learning opportunities. To lead teams effectively you will need to give them opportunities to make mistakes, and be prepared to clean up the mess.

Coach your leaders

Jesus would often take his leaders aside to teach them or reflect with them on the ministry they were involved in, as well as on their own life. We have a coaching system with our youth leaders where someone sits with them and discusses how they are going with the youth ministry's vision, how they are going in their own personal life and walk with Jesus, and what resources they need to keep doing the work that God has set before them. The combination of these three areas results in a holistic approach to developing leaders.

Look for new opportunities

Jesus was not afraid to give his team new tasks to do (Matthew Chapter 10). There are plenty of opportunities around the local church that are ripe for young leaders to step into. A number of great initiatives have started in our youth ministry that could not have started if it was left to me. Leaders on your team have skills and passions you don't have. Look for ways to encourage them to use their skills and be prepared to cheer them along and learn from them.

At the end of the day, your team will probably be a bit like Jesus' team. Some members will grow in leaps and bounds and do great things for the kingdom. Others will lead for a time, and (realistically) some will turn on you and even on the cause. The challenge, though, is to not be discouraged and to keep actively building the team.

10. Parents

Some of the most satisfying moments in youth ministry occur when parents express their thanks for the ways youth ministry has assisted their child or family. On the flip side, one of my strongest memories is of a parent expressing her dissatisfaction with a particular event at which her son was quite seriously injured. Here's my advice.

Parents are unavoidable

Regardless of your approach to parents, they are unavoidable participants in youth ministry. With a little wisdom they are your greatest asset! Too often younger youth leaders think that parents get in the way; parents can quickly be positioned as the enemy of youth ministry. Most parents, despite what the teenager may say, actually want what is good for their children. With a little thought and work, combined with a parent-friendly attitude, your parents can be the 'cheerleaders' rather than the 'fear leaders' of your youth ministry.

Parents are people too

Parents have real lives full of real joys and real struggles. Make sure that you take time to listen to and develop relationships with parents.

Developing an understanding of their life and their thoughts about their children gives you an appreciation of some of the decisions they make, and gives them a sense of respect and regard for the ministry. Passages like Deuteronomy 6 and Ephesians 6 speak of the responsibility parents have in the raising of their children and of the need for children to honour their parents. How does your youth ministry promote this idea?

Partner with parents

As parents are involved in the youth ministry, they develop a greater sense of participation and the youth see them as the help rather than the enemy. Our youth ministry has a variety of roles for parents. Be wise about where you use parents, and how you brief them, but give them opportunities to appropriately partner with the youth ministry. Some great ideas include: safety, drivers, house parents, special events crew and elements of youth leader training. If you fail to provide opportunities for parents to be involved you may find them creating their own opportunities.

Find parents who promote

As the relationships develop and a mutual respect is obtained, you will find parents promote the youth ministry. We find this particularly with our annual youth camp. There is a lot of distrust of churches in our culture, and a lot of protective parenting (both are understandable in our culture). Allowing your child to attend a week long church youth camp is a big deal for Aussie parents. But our parent body sells it to new parents. The parents trust the ministry. They see the value of the camp. They have become promoters. What an asset!

Plan with parents

This is the most threatening, but perhaps the most beneficial. My youngest child is just finishing her time in our youth ministry. I have had over 25 years of experience in youth ministry but the last 9 years, in which my own children have been participants, have taught me the most about healthy youth ministry. Have a look around your parent body, particularly if you have some parents who are promoters. How can you involve them in your planning? How can your youth ministry benefit from their wisdom?

Your experience of parents in youth ministry will be largely deter-mined by your attitude and approach to them. Foster a positive and healthy one, and delight in the fruit it produces for the ministry.

11. You and senior church leaders

The relationship with your church's team, senior pastor or minister will, to a large extent, be the most influential relationship within your leadership team. While they may not serve in the youth ministry itself, their power and interest in the youth ministry is paramount.

Remember you are there to support them in the ministry of the church

The quicker you realise this, the more helpful it will be both for you and the youth ministry. The youth ministry fits under the goals and pur-poses of the whole church - and so do you as the youth leader/pastor. While at times it is frustrating and humbling, you benefit from not hav-ing to worry about a broad range of issues and politics within the church. Appreciate the freedom to get on with ministry and work out ways to support your senior leader.

Understand the senior leader and how they tick

Each senior leader I have worked with is different. Some I have more naturally connected with than others. The more I know and understand them, the easier it is to work with them. Spend time engaging with their interests and passions. Understand their ministry and life journey. Learn to understand them as a human, as a fellow being created in the image of God. Remember that often the best way to get through personal or ministry challenges is to act lovingly; that may be as simple as bringing them a coffee, sending an encouraging text or acknowledging the work they are doing.

Bring ideas and concerns to the senior leader humbly

You will have different ideas than the senior leader. The senior leader won't like them all and may not even like the best ones. I have found that when I am able to bring ideas in humility it ALWAYS goes better. It doesn't mean the ideas are all accepted (though a humble presentation might help or allow for some tweaking of an idea), but it does mean my attitude is checked and Godly. In turn, that attitude enables me to continue as a healthy and constructive team member even if I am personally disappointed by the end result of the idea presented. As I look back I remember a significant team meeting where I raised an idea that has been a catalyst for change in our church. I remember consciously thinking that I needed to raise the idea in such a way that if there was no energy for it at the end of the meeting, I would drop it permanently.

Disagree in private

Embarrassingly, I have disagreed publicly with my senior leader. I am talking about the big things here, not discussions about the new choice of colour for a wall. I have come to learn that while what I disagreed about may have been right (sometimes it will be and sometimes it won't), the *way* I approached the issue was unhelpful. Anything that is particularly close to the heart of the senior leader, or that may reflect negatively on the leader, or is actually about your relationship with the leader, should be taken up privately with the leader.

Endure

You will have some good times and some tough times with your senior leader. Endure lovingly through the tough times, actively seeking a healthy relationship. Every time you have to endure, remember your senior leader will at times have to endure with you.

Chapter 2
Nathan Chiroma from Nigeria

My chapter is dedicated to Dr Iliya Majam for mentoring me in youth ministry.

1. My background and how I got into youth ministry

I grew up in a Christian family. My father was a missionary to the Muslims in Northern Nigeria for 40 years, so I was surrounded by God and the church from the very beginning. But I just went through the motions of doing 'Christian things' at first because I thought that was all I needed to do to be saved. I didn't know Christ, I just knew about Him.

During my high school days I found myself searching for purpose and meaning in people and also in myself. Whether that was my friends or in relationships, I poured my whole heart into them. I also became very fixated on myself and my image. I became very consumed with what people thought of me and I wanted to be accepted by the world.

My dramatic conversion experience happened at my lowest point when I was alone and afraid. It was 1979, when God used my Sunday school teacher to draw me to Himself. One fateful Saturday evening I was punished at home for an offence I didn't commit. My younger brother committed the offence and denied it; as I was the only other person who could have done it I was heavily disciplined by my mother. On Sunday morning the lesson from my Sunday school teacher was about the punishment that Jesus took on our behalf. The lesson made perfect sense to me considering my experience the day before. Growing up in a Christian home, I knew what I had to do. I knew that Jesus could save me if I just let Him. So I did. I then shared my new faith with my family, and my mother taught me how to follow Jesus.

Since knowing Him, God has shown me that being a Christian involves ministering to others using my spiritual gifts. I started working with the Sunday school and after high school I went to Bible College to study for a certificate in theology to enable me work to with young people. I was called to full time ministry in 1989 as a youth pastor in the city of Wurno, Nigeria and later on served as a youth minister in Nairobi, Kenya. After completing a Master's Degree in Divinity in 2001, I was called to teach youth ministry at Evangelical Church of West Africa (ECWA) Seminary in the city of Jos, Nigeria whilst at the same time serving as the youth pastor in my local congregation.

I met my wife Jane in Kenya in 1999 and we got married in 2001. God has blessed our marriage with two sons (Nasuri, age 11 and Namiri, age 10). My wife and I moved to South Africa in 2007 to obtain our PhD's and while there God opened the door for me to work part time as a student minister with Stellenbosch Baptist Church in the city of Stellenbosch.

2. Looking after your own soul

One of my greatest struggles when I moved into full time vocational youth ministry was balance. Most youth workers struggle with balance in ministry! How do you balance your personal life, professional life, and times spent with young people? I had to decide between how to say "no" to some commitments in order to spend quality time with God or spend quality time with my family. Moreover, I was under a lot of pressure to work with the youth, and at the same time to keep up with preaching, my school visits, hospital visits, etc. In the midst of all these challenges, after some few years of struggle and a lot of consultation with other experienced youth workers, I eventually found two things that are very helpful in striking the needed balance in my life and ministry. They are setting goals and having a personal support network.

Setting goals

Often I found myself busy with the 'urgent' and neglecting the 'important'. I found that setting goals helps me to prioritise and differentiate between the two. The story of Mary and Martha in the gospels is always a constant reminder: Martha was busy with the urgent, while Mary was busy with the important. Jesus reminded Martha that she was worried about so many things, yet one thing is really important and Mary had chosen that, spending time with the Master. As a youth worker my time with God comes first before ministry. I am now conscious of the fact that God is more interested in who I *am* for him than in what I *do* for him; hence, I make it a priority and first goal to spend time with God.

Personal support network

Thriving youth workers gain strength from others who encourage, challenge, pray for, and believe in them; these kinds of people became stewards of God's grace in my life. I found out that the more intentional I am in building these relationships, the more God can move through them to strengthen me for the long haul. These relationships are typified by mutual discipleship, holding each other accountable for faithful living, accountability in ministry and family, peer mentoring and upward mentoring, where we receive advice and counsel from someone more experienced than us. I realized that no matter how long I have been in ministry I find a lot of benefit from ongoing relationships with mentors. Connections to people who have more experience, wisdom, and grace have helped me quash many rash decisions before they backfire.

3. Singleness, marriage and children

Dealing with singleness, marriage and having children is a very complex issue in my community. These are topics that are not often discussed openly; they are seen as taboo, and are meant to be kept a secret. My journey regarding marriage, family and children is an even more complex one because of the various expectations of a youth pastor in my society. Pastors can be seen as being either superhuman, or poor. During our time at Bible College we were encouraged not to date a girl in the church where we were ministering because of the assumption that as a pastor you will lose the respect of the congregation; so my philosophy of marriage and dating was built upon that.

I met my wife in Kenya where I was studying for my Master of Divinity degree. She was leading a kids' Bible club and we agreed to start dating after a few months. However, we were both afraid of what our parents and other extended family thought. It is not only a cross-cultural marriage but also a marriage across two countries. We faced a lot of opposition, especially from my wife's parents because I am a Nigerian (Nigerians have a bad reputation in several countries). But after a lot of prayer and consultation we both received the consent of our parents to get married.

We got married in 2001 and lived in Kenya for one year before moving back to Nigeria. My wife went through considerable culture shock as she adapted to marriage and family culture in my country. The wife is seen as belonging to the clan and not just to the man she is married to. As such she is often referred to as 'our wife'. Secondly, it is expected that as a couple you will have a child within a year of your marriage. When my wife and I said we will have children after two years it was seen as going against the culture and my wife was at one point depressed about the whole situation. But through the help of our mentor she eventually recovered.

Ministry demands on me as a pastor also led to challenges in our marriage, especially in Nigeria. The pastor is thought to have the answer to all of life's problems, and many times I am called upon in the middle of the night to deal with an issue that needs counselling, at the expense of my family. Through the help of God and my ministry mentors I am gradually dealing with that challenge and trying my best to strike a balance between my family life and my ministry life.

My advice to other youth pastors is that they must strive to set their priorities correctly: God, family and then ministry. Youth pastors in my context must come to terms with the truth that they are only human. They must not let society dictate how they run their lives and ministry. I will encourage them to spend a lot of time dating their intended spouse and to keep that up even after they are married.

4. Organising yourself and your ministry

I struggled a lot with organization in my early years of youth ministry. There were times when I had double bookings for functions or with people as a result of not being organized. I was people and program driven and I struggled to say 'No' because I didn't want to offend people. However, I was blessed to work with a senior pastor who taught me the skill of organization. I had to submit my weekly appointments and weekly schedule for discussion every Monday, and that was the beginning of me becoming more organized in both my life and ministry. Later on when I got married my wife also helped me a lot.

One key lesson that I learned about organization is the act of delegation. When I started to delegate aspects of my ministry to young people I was mentoring it became a lot easier for me to be organized. At first I was afraid that the young people would not be able to carry out the assignments the way I wanted, but they proved me wrong - all they needed was supervision. At this stage I am thankful to mentors, cell phones, and ipads that help me organize my life and ministry with more ease.

My advice to new volunteers, part time or full time youth workers about organizing themselves and their ministry is to learn the act of delegation. We need a balance between our ministry and our lives in order to be effective. I would also encourage you to have accountability partners who will constantly remind you of the difference between what is urgent and what is important. Remember that youth ministry is *for* the young people and *by* the young people.

5. Keeping your evangelism edge sharp

Evangelism is one of the primary strengths in my youth ministry. I do not see evangelism as an end in itself, but as a means to discipleship which I believe is key in youth ministry. Without evangelism, discipleship does not happen because an integral part of growing young people to maturity is learning to share the good news. Evangelism accelerates the growth of disciples in youth ministry.

I plan evangelism with the core youth group (these are often the leaders that I have mentored and discipled). We often start by going away for a weekend of prayer, evaluation and planning. We will then look at the key areas or schools where we will focus our outreach, and the form of evangelism (this includes the location, types of literature to use, studying the youth in the area, etc). We then communicate this to the church leadership for prayer and support.

After several years in my youth ministry I figured that young people were always afraid to share their faith because they are afraid of rejection, or don't know how to do it. So I help my young people share their faith by using their personal testimony (sharing how their life was before the gospel, how they are now that they know the gospel, and what they are hoping for). I often encourage them to make Jesus the centre of the testimony. People can argue about many things, but personal testimony is always hard to deny. I also help my young people to share their faith through a direct approach to evangelism, e.g. "You must be born again" (John 3), an indirect approach, e.g. "Give me water to drink" (John 4), and a question approach, e.g. "Do you understand what you are reading?" (Acts 8). We practice a lot and encourage each other before we go out. We normally go out in pairs on the days that we do door to door outreach. Truth is more often caught than taught.

Other tools that I use include the Youth for Christ's *Three-Story Evangelism*: my story, the other person's story and God's story. I have found it very helpful and it keeps the focus on reaching out to the other person and giving them a chance to share their story. I also use sports, social media (Facebook especially), short mission trips, prison visits and social action in the community. I find that young people are always excited to use their abilities.

6. Communicating with youth

Early in my youth ministry days I would always try to find a seminar and conference on 'How to teach young people'. I later realized that the more I attended those seminars and conferences the more confused I became! During a second year class in my Master of Divinity degree I finally found a balance on what and how to teach young people. I adopted the basic method from the life of Paul in Athens (Acts 17), starting with what they know and creating common ground. In the part of Africa where I come from, most adults assume that young people don't know anything and must just sit down and listen to adults. However, after working with young people in many parts of Africa I came to realize that they know a lot!

I always start by asking them questions about what they know, and then from there move on to what they don't know. My aim is to always reach the head, the heart and the hands. I try to give them some cognitive knowledge (the head) regarding the topic, then move down to the affective level (the heart), e.g. what does the lesson has to do with me? Then, finally, the hands - what can I do with the message that I have learnt? I use mainly thematic Bible study methods and do expository teaching of books of the Bible, relating it to the daily issues young people are facing. I apply the 'Book, Look, and Took' principle as well. We take the book of the Bible, we look at it together, and then see what we can take (took) from it together.

I have found some of the most effective ways to teach young people in my context are through modelling, storytelling, case studies, drama and outings. In modelling I often invite to the group a renowned Christian leader, sports person or anyone that is considered successful in the community, and ask them to share with the young people. Beforehand I will often highlight to the speaker the passage of Scripture we are studying so they can make a link to their story. Storytelling is very important in the African culture, so I include various stories that bring home the passage we are studying with young people.

Case studies involve taking a life event and asking the young people to relate it to their life and to the passage we are studying. Many of the young people like to talk about the events that made the headlines during the week; we will discuss them and see how relevant they are to our life and community. I also often ask young people to stage a drama on the topic of discussion. I have found out over the years that young people will always remember a Bible passage that was dramatized for them. We also have outings to correctional services, orphanages, juvenile homes, and old age homes in order to help, observe and interact. After the visit we will come back and discuss the result of our outings and how it relates to our Bible lessons.

7. Pastoral care of young people

My theological foundation for pastoral care of young people is inextricably linked to the biblical image of the shepherd. "The Lord is my shepherd", the psalmist declares (Psalm 23:1). "I am the good shepherd", Jesus informs his hearers (John 10:11). In my context and experience pastoral care for the youth can take many forms. However, I will focus on the following.

Worship

In providing pastoral care for youth I always want to help them focus on God first and not me as the caregiver. Helping them engage in meaningful worship helps prevent them from casting their gaze on me as the youth pastor and instead casts their focus on God. The act of pastoral care for the youth reminds me that the ministry of pastoral care is grounded in the act of worship. I strongly believe in what John Calvin wrote in his Institutes of the Christian Religion (1559), "It is certain that man never achieves a clear knowledge of himself unless he has first looked upon God's face, and then descends from contemplating Him to scrutinize himself" (Institutes 1:1:2). Knowledge of ourselves is utterly bound up with our knowledge of God. I help young people to immerse themselves in God through worship as a foundation to understanding the Good Shepherd.

Healing

In providing pastoral care for youth in my context I also focus on healing. Many of the young people I am working with need healing from various experiences in their lives. I often use the redemption model of journeying along with the young people in order to provide them with healing that only God can provide. I believe that healing is a biblical sign of God's redemptive work. I remind the young people that all healing is part of God's work of salvation, and that God is the ultimate agent of healing. Indeed, one of the Hebrew names for God is Jehovah-Rapha, which means, 'The Lord who heals'. Often I allow them to narrate their stories and see how their story fits into God's story. I remember the particular case of a young lady who was raped by three policemen. She struggled to forgive and to trust anyone. Using the redemption model I encourage her to see God, even in her deep hurt, and thankfully today she is a public speaker and is busy working with other women who have gone through similar experiences.

Counselling

In providing pastoral care for youth, I also engage them through counselling. Youth pastoral counselling for me takes place in the context of a pastoral relationship, which itself is embedded in the life of a pastoral community, i.e. the church. I utilize the tools of Scripture, ritual, prayer and community support as appropriate. My focus is to have a strong faith component. This is consistent with the focus of youth pastoral care as 'the cure of the soul'.

8. Working with schools

When I started youth work in Nigeria, access to schools by youth workers was not a problem. However, in the last 15 years, because of religious sensitivity, things are changing. In the Southern and the Eastern part of Nigeria there seems to still be easy to access to public schools. However, in the Northern part where I come from things are getting a bit difficult. By law, public schools have to provide religious education for both Muslims and Christians. There is provision for religious groups like the Muslim Students Society and the Fellowship of Christian Students. As youth workers we often gain access to schools through those who teach religion there.

My experience

In Nigeria, Kenya and in South Africa I worked mainly among Christian schools and in some public schools. It usually started with an invitation from a teacher to speak on a specific occasion like graduation, chapel hour, etc. After that I would follow up with a request to do other things in that particular school. I have been involved in sex education, HIV/AIDS awareness, book clubs, volunteer tutoring and as a soccer coach. I used this involvement as a tool to reach out to the young people.

As the years passed I saw an opportunity to connect with parents who often come to either drop off their kids or fetch their kids. That resulted in a program I called 'Parents Connect'. We agreed to meet first with fathers and sons over breakfast once in a month. Later we had parenting seminars each term for both parents. The most interesting encounter for me was when a girl who attended our summer camp went home and told her parents that they should ask me to organise a family camp; the parents fully sponsored one for the community and over 30 families attended.

My advice to youth workers in Nigeria and elsewhere

1. Make sure you create intentional friendships with school teachers, especially in public schools in your community.
2. Make sure you involve parents in the community and parents that are part of a Parent Teachers Association (PTA) or similar - get the parents involved in their children's lives through the various activities you plan in schools and ask them to volunteer.
3. Build partnerships with other organizations that are working among young people in schools, e.g. Cru (formerly known as Campus Crusade for Christ), Youth for Christ, Fellowship of Christian Students, etc.
4. Get your churches involved in whatever capacity they can in schools ministry; often churches are not involved because they

are not aware of the potential in it.

5. Make sure you create time to hang out in school with the kids from your youth group in church.

9. Leading a team and developing others

Leadership is a very important aspect of youth ministry. My personal philosophy of youth ministry leadership is 'youth ministry for the young people by the young people'. This makes me more of a facilitator and developer of leaders. I strongly believe that, given the right modelling and the right space, young people are able to lead.

The first move in leading and developing others is selecting a group of 5 young people who will serve as the leadership committee. I meet with them every week to plan, to pray and to prepare for the entire ministry. They are responsible for the day to day affairs of the youth ministry and I also meet with them regularly to evaluate their leadership. This group normally serves for a period of three years, after which I will select another 5 and run with them. The earlier 5 who finished their term as core leaders will be assigned to lead smaller groups and be responsible for the development of other leaders through discipleship and mentoring.

The second aspect of my leadership is what I call the leadership constellation. These are adults and volunteers willing to invest their time and energy in young people's lives. The first step is making sure that the adults are connected to each other as well as to the young people. The recruiting of these adults and volunteers usually comes up at least six months before a new year of youth group ministry. Once I have these adults and volunteers, I regularly communicate with them, give them job descriptions, behavioral covenants, and an accountability structure. I also make sure I affirm and encourage them regularly.

The third element is what I call 'Equipping the Next Potential Leaders'. These are often younger people who have the potential for leadership and I will engage them through mentoring and discipleship. These are the young people who I consider will feed into the core leadership of the youth ministry in the future. I engage them in leadership training opportunities so as to build up leadership confidence in them. This is crucial for youth ministry in my context because young people are often not considered for leadership and are looked down upon. They often develop an inferiority complex when it comes to leadership. The main material

I use in mentoring them are those Scriptures focusing on leaders in the Old Testament and the story of David.

The key thing for me in all the various leadership stages is to give young people power to carry out ministry. It is all about giving them the opportunity to learn from their successes and failures; this will help them to develop their God-given potential as leaders.

10. Parents

In my context the myth is that youth ministry is for pastors, youth workers and all those who are called to work with younger people. As a youth pastor I was taught to believe that I am to work with young people in isolation, not in the community. Thankfully, through one of my mentors, Dr. Iliya Majams, I was helped to understand that living out the power of salvation in the lives of young people is not a solitary enterprise. It is a concerted effort by a group a people who put forward a different idea of what life ought to be. This can offer youth a formidable way in which to challenge the forces of conformity. I was able to understand that young people belong to God, and that in Scripture the primary responsibility of raising kids is not in the hands of the church but in the hands of the family. This gave me a different focus for my youth ministry, especially in the area of engaging parents and involving them to make it a family based youth ministry. I involved parents in the following ways:

Training and volunteering

I hold parenting seminars once a quarter, especially with the parents of teenagers I am working with. The purpose of these is to highlight the synergy that takes place when parents and youth pastors work together. This training also equips them to complement my work with young people at home, so that the focus of youth ministry is emphasized on both fronts. It equips parents to see the need to communicate with their kids and be the primary spiritual mentors to them.

I involve parents as volunteers in most of our programs, especially during our camps and student nights. Parents will be involved in the planning and execution of the programs. Some parents plays the role of security personnel during camps, some will help in the kitchen and others will help in leading small groups.

Prayer team

I recruit parents who will intercede for the youth ministry. We meet once a month to share the joys and the challenges of the ministry, and to pray for it. Many parents find fulfilment in praying not only for their own kids but all the kids in the church. I have come to feel, and see, the power of God working amongst young people as a result of the prayers of those parents. At the end of the year I invite the praying parents to come and meet with the youth group; many kids will either be shocked or amazed that their parents are part of the people praying for them.

Fundraising

I involve parents in fund raising for specific projects in youth ministry. This is because our church tradition does not assign much of a budget for youth ministry. Many parents joyfully contribute and help to raise funds for projects in youth ministry. This has given them satisfaction and ownership of the ministry, and as a result many of them have come to realize that the work is not just for the youth pastors but it is for the entire congregation.

11. You and senior church leaders

Serving alongside a senior leader and leadership team in youth ministry can be both a challenge and opportunity. I struggled a lot during my early days in youth ministry since most of the senior ministers I worked with saw me as a threat, not as an asset to develop. At one point I was close to quitting, but thankfully again one of my mentors encouraged me and gave me some hints. Over the years I have learnt a few more.

Firstly, working with a senior leader and leadership team, one needs to communicate well and communicate clearly. I discovered that most senior leaders do not want to be caught off guard, so commit to being thorough and make sure your senior leader and leadership team know about the major events and programs in your ministry.

Second, try your best to invite your senior leader to your key events. Be deliberate and think through a couple of different ways your senior leader and team leadership can contribute to your ministry. It may be something as simple as a brief presence at volunteer training or a short message to the teenagers, or it may be as much as showing up to a camp or retreat.

Third, as a matter of principle, never talk about your senior leader or your leadership team behind their backs. This is a matter of integrity! Do not openly disagree with your senior leader or talk negatively about them to members of your congregation or your youth group. There are avenues for you to share your deep concerns, but that should remain behind closed doors and surrounded with prayer. At all possible times show the congregation and your team that you are moving forward in the same direction. This is especially crucial in situations where you have a denominational hierarchy.

Fourth, when and where possible discuss on a regular basis your plans and vision for youth ministry. Keep your senior leadership team up-to-date on what you are thinking and the direction in which you want to go. Keep them informed and value their input. Remember, they are also 'in the know' about the congregation you are working with and they can give you broader perspective to your youth ministry plans.

Finally, always be prepared to offer your senior leader and leadership team help, especially when they seem to be overloaded. The temptation for many of us as youth pastors is to think we are the hardest working people in the church, and we may miss opportunities to help our senior leaders. The truth is that some of them are often overloaded with ministry and on top of this they have a personal life as well. Even though your schedule may be as overloaded as your senior leaders, it will send a huge message if you offer to help out when you can.

Chapter 3
Anne De Jesus-Ardina from The Philippines

My chapter is dedicated to those who taught me well, my professors in youth ministry: Dan Jessen, Len Kageler, Mark Lamport, Dave Rahn, Scott Welch, Bill Hodgson, Les Cristie, Rick Dunn, Fred Gingrich, Tenny Li and Paul Borthwick.

1. My background and how I got into youth ministry

The Philippine archipelago, consisting of 7,107 islands (only 2,000 of which are inhabited) is where I make my home. Although an Asian country influenced by its neighbors - Malaysia, Indonesia, China, Japan, and India - much of its culture has been borrowed from the Spanish and Americans, having been under their rule for three centuries and almost five decades, respectively. The Philippines first earned world fame when our compatriots ousted the dictator president Marcos through the peaceful 'Edsa Revolution'. We are known to be a friendly, hospitable, religious and resilient people, able to gracefully bear the onslaught of natural and manmade disasters.

Our last name De Jesus, which means "Of Jesus" is very apt. Many of my family have been in vocational ministry: my great-grandfather, grandparents, parents, uncles/aunts, siblings, cousins, myself, my husband, and now our son Mikhael. Since my grandfather's time, our family clan has belonged to the Christian and Missionary Alliance Churches of the Philippines, a member of the denomination founded by a man from Canada called Albert Benjamin Simpson. We believe in Jesus Christ as Saviour, Sanctifier, Healer and Coming King, and still carry our founder's vision for worldwide missions.

Set apart

As the only girl, and eldest of four children, the first ten years of my life were like a 'cloistered community' consisting of the pastor's house, the church, and a Christian school. At age five I asked Jesus to be my Saviour during a church meeting for children. Growing up as a pastor's kid likewise gave me the opportunity to be well grounded in the Word, be involved in church activities and learn from those more mature in the faith. Perhaps because of my constant exposure to the ministry, as early as age ten, I was determined that I would become a minister...even when I went through the stages of wanting to be a teacher, nurse, stewardess, TV broadcaster and journalist! The desire to serve God in a full-time capacity had been planted in my heart since I was young. It was cultivated as I grew older and saw the lost world's need of a Saviour. Working in a church/Christian setting was not new to me. I not only felt comfortable doing it, but I enjoyed it as well. Deep in my heart, I knew without any doubt that I was set apart as God's servant.

A clear call

After graduating from Ebenezer Bible College and Seminary in Zamboanga City, Philippines (where I also met my husband) we ministered at a church before going back to the Seminary to teach. It wasn't until I decided to pursue a Master's degree that the clear call of specialising in youth ministry surfaced. When I considered what my passion was, the need in our country (approximately 60% of the population under the age of 30), as well as where my gifts/talents would be most maximized, youth ministry was the most logical choice. I also remembered my turbulent days as a youth and how it was important to have significant adults (some youth ministers) in my life to guide me. Besides teaching youth ministry at the Alliance Graduate School since 2001, I have also been a youth minister in four of our Metro Manila local churches since 1985. I have been Metro Manila District Youth Director and a member/consultant of the Alliance Youth Philippines board.

2. Looking after your own soul

As a person in the people-helping, soul-caring ministry to youth, you will find that you need to help yourself and take care of your own soul as well.

Not just a textbook

After graduating from Bible College I realised I had been using the Bible as just another textbook, rather than God's Word that would guide, instruct and inspire me. Thus, when I took my Master's degree at Seminary I made sure that despite all the coursework that needed to be done, which often required reading the Bible, I set aside separate time to read the Bible because of what it is: God's Word, and not just another textbook. This has been a helpful practice in youth ministry as I plan my preaching and teaching to youth. I do not treat the Bible as a mere 're-source' but as a powerful two-edged sword that can transform the lives of the youth I minister to. We probably all have our favourite version of the Bible, but reading the Bible through in another version each time can make it more interesting and enriching. Thankfully, we have many resources on the internet for personal Bible study, but it is also good to make personal notes, even jotting down questions.

Get away - just like the young people do!

I make a point of going on an out-of-town spiritual retreat (on my own or with a group) at least once a year. If our young people benefit from attending camps and retreats, we too, as youth ministers, can benefit from them as well! During the first five years of ministry I almost burned out; it manifested itself physically, emotionally and spiritually. I realised there were two main reasons for this: 1) I was a people pleaser and could not say "NO", and 2) I didn't have a day off or vacations. From that time on, I realised that if I wanted to survive in youth ministry, I had to set aside time for a regular day off during the week, as well as regular vacations, and time for spiritual retreats. And yes...say "NO" sometimes.

Journaling, friends and other books

A consistent prayer life is something I'm striving to achieve. Using a prayer journal, where I have people or concerns to pray for every day of the week, helps me in this area. To make sure that I don't forget, especially when I hear of a problem and I don't have my journal with me, I make it a point to pray right there and then.

For a long time I felt I was too busy to meet up with friends and colleagues in the ministry. But I realised that it is quite beneficial to have a group of people who are travelling the same 'road' as you, going through the same struggles, and experiencing the same challenges and joys. It's wonderful to grow and learn together, as well as encourage and build each other up in the faith and ministry.

Read devotional and inspirational books that will help you grow spiritually. One of the resources that has greatly helped me as a youth minister is my professor Paul Borthwick's classic book *Feeding Your Forgotten Soul*. I use it regularly to mentor my youth ministry students. Each time I read/teach it, I am reminded not to neglect the care of my own soul.

3. Singleness, marriage and children

Filipino youth are now copying the western trend of marrying later. Since many of our young ladies are somewhat 'liberated' compared to our Asian counterparts, have strong personalities, land good jobs, and are quite smart...some young men may feel threatened or inadequate. Thus, some of these ladies end up being single and focus on their careers and caring for their elderly parents. On the other hand, young men feel pressured to acquire a house, a car, and save up for a grand wedding before even considering marriage. Thus, some men likewise remain single.

As a youth minister, I am expected to guide young people in coming up with criteria for the 'right one' as well as give advice on BGR: Boy-Girl Relationships. We are often the go-to person, a 'Love Doctor' when young people are plagued with problems of the heart!

Traditionally, after a man proposes to his girlfriend and they make plans to get married, he does a 'Pamanhikan' (literally 'entreat'), where he and his parents visit the girlfriend's family at their house to ask for her hand in marriage. Although an old practice, some still use a third party to act as a mediator. The youth pastor may be asked to play this special role.

Marriage

Having been both single and married in youth ministry, I have seen the advantages and disadvantages of both. As a single lady youth minister, it was a challenge to minister to young men without it being awkward, especially when some of them would show romantic interest...or would misinterpret my pastoral care for something else. So I made sure I kept a safe distance, literally and figuratively. I made it clear that I was their 'Ate' (older sister).

If it's your calling, get married as soon as possible. Being the eternal eligible bachelor/bachelorette is not going to help much in youth ministry. Young people look up to us, and we may not be able to handle that much attention and adoration.

When I got married, I was able to relax a bit more, but not too much, knowing that temptation will always be lurking. And although I try to be as approachable, personable and relational as possible, I maintain my boundaries. It helps when you introduce the youth to your spouse, talk about them often, and refer youth of the opposite sex to them, especially for counselling regarding delicate matters.

Children

Having just one child gave us the opportunity to be more mobile, taking our son along almost anywhere we went, providing for him as best we could, and giving him the care and attention he needed. I'm not saying this is for everyone...if I had the chance to have more children, I'd still grab it. So involve your children in your ministry, even while they are still young. Since he was three years old, we took our son with us for ministry trips, youth camps and retreats, discipleship training, seminars, preaching and speaking engagements, and staff meetings. The result? He's now a youth pastor himself!

4. Organising yourself and your ministry

'Organized clutter' - that describes my office, and it is a reflection of my paradoxical life. There is lots of 'stuff' in my life—hectic activities (which I've labelled 'hectivities'), appointments, 'to-do' lists, simultaneous projects...but I manage to keep things under control most of the time. Being a pastor's kid I'm used to constant change and chaos. In fact, I think I thrive on it. I have slowly learned how to deal with these and manage my life.

It wasn't always so. There were times in the past when I missed meetings and appointments. So much so that I earned the reputation of being forgetful, even as a young person. I would submit my college papers late and fail to get the grade I aspired to. During my junior year (second last year) of college, I decided to start taking control of my life and develop ways to be better organized.

Easier single or married?

Many times, it's difficult to balance our lives, especially when everything comes to a head. Sometimes we even need to organize our organizing! Single people may think it's easier to manage their lives, being less complicated without a spouse and kids. Conversely, married people may find life overwhelming. Having been a single youth minister, and now a married one, I know that this is not always the case. Single people may assume they have all the time in the world and so become lazy. Married people know they have limited time for each activity and so can often be more intentional, finishing each piece of work in its allotted time frame.

Not everyone is a planner (and not everyone is a finisher!). Some people like to be spontaneous, insisting that their creative juices flow during the 11th hour. Fine...sometimes true. However, the downside of these last minute frenzies are often not worth it: forgotten or missed appointments, burning the midnight oil to beat the deadline, irritability, frustration, panic attacks, ulcers, and over-used adrenalin.

My tips for organizing life and ministry:

- Use a planner with a yearly overview, monthly pages and weekly spreadsheets.
- Prayerfully plan for the year, quarter, month, week and day.
- Plot out regular activities.
- Pencil in appointments/deadlines in your planner as they come in.
- Intentionally make time for important things: God, family, friends, ministry, self, etc.
- Decide your priorities and non-negotiables. Learn to say "NO" when requests don't fit in.
- Allow for ebb and flow, balancing work and rest.
- Debunk the Messiah-complex-Lone-Ranger-attitude: work with a team.
- D.E.L.E.G.A.T.E., making sure each one knows their ministry description to avoid duplication or unaccomplished tasks.
- Make use of media and technology to facilitate communication and follow up.
- Sweat the small stuff, i.e. pay attention to detail. If you don't then

things can creep up and pile up until they become too much to handle.

- Mom's right: "Have a place for everything, and everything in its place".
- When you've done your part, leave the rest to God...after all, He's in control!

5. Keeping your evangelism edge sharp

Like many youth workers, and even pastors (and I guess Christians in general), evangelism is not my greatest strength. Neither is it a strong area in most of our churches. Sometimes it is a sporadic event; sometimes just an annual item in the Church or youth ministry calendar. It is rarely a lifestyle of every church member. But just because it is not something I'm especially good at, it doesn't give me (or any of us) an excuse to shirk our Christian responsibility.

It has become quite challenging these days because of postmodernist philosophy, where we are expected to be 'inclusive', taught to be 'tolerant' and not discriminate, be 'politically correct', and avoid 'absolutes'. This is especially true in our country, which is the proverbial melting pot of people coming from various ethnic and national backgrounds, with our respective religions and beliefs: Roman Catholics, Liberal Christians, Evangelicals, Charismatics/Pentecostals (often differentiating themselves from Evangelicals), International and Nationalized Cults, Muslims, Buddhists, Taoists, Confucianists, Animists, New Agers, and Syncretists. To be seen as pushing your belief on others, or attempting to convert them, could brand you as a bigot at the least and could even result in persecution and assassination at most.

Although most of my dealings have been with church youth, we do have the opportunity to witness to others outside our church. Some non-parochial and public schools are open for Religious Instruction, and I have had the chance to teach in such a school. Others welcome people who teach Values Education, and we use biblical teachings and principles as the foundation. In fact, I have co-written Values Education textbooks which are being used in schools all over the Philippines.

Our church has successfully used creative means such as sport, basketball for boys and volleyball for girls, to win over the community youth. Music is a great way to attract Filipino youth, so sponsoring band concerts and contests are always a hit. Evangelistic retreats and camps work well where we have guest speakers who are not only great with youth but good in evangelism too. Cabin counsellors or small group leaders are at hand to talk with young people who have become Christians.

But most importantly, we disciple our church youth so that they can share their faith and disciple their peers as well. Training them and equipping them with various evangelistic tools has helped them gain confidence: e.g. Bridge Illustration, Wordless Book, Evangelism Explosion (Youth Edition), The Four Spiritual Laws, Evangecube, and other creative means using simple props. One Christmas I made 'Wordless Wooden Bead Bracelets' for our youth to wear and use for evangelism.

6. Communicating with youth

When I started teaching youth I made the mistake of dealing with topics that were sure to be a hit with them: LCM (Love, Courtship and Marriage) and Peers. Filipinos, even the youth, value relationships so talks about family relationships proved to be interesting as well. Besides, I enjoyed topics on relationships, and had somehow gained the reputation of being an expert of sorts. Perhaps the reason I stuck with these topics for a long time was because I felt safe and confident with them.

Later, I 'graduated' to what I thought would be an improvement by varying my topics according to monthly themes. I would plot out the year's teaching plan by having a theme for the year, quarter, month, then weekly topics. It was a success for a while...until I ran out of themes and so kept repeating the usual themes, e.g. 'New Leaf' or 'Goal Setting' for the New Year, 'Love' for February, 'Graduation' for March, etc.

It wasn't until I was taking my Master's studies in Youth Ministry that our visiting professor Scott Welch shared with us a novel (for us) idea to teach through the Bible, not just dwelling on topics that young people wanted to hear (their felt needs), and the accompanying verses of Scripture passages that normally went along with them, but teaching the whole Bible (their real need). He proposed a three year cycle since that's how long the average young person stays in a youth group. Our Filipino educational system is a bit different, so I opted for a five year cycle.

Another visiting professor, Dr Dan Jessen, also informed us that young people nowadays are biblically illiterate. Not quite believing him (I thought maybe Filipino youth had an edge because our country is touted as 'the only Christian country in Asia' and fifth in the world), I gave my youth a Bible quiz by Terry Hall in his book *Getting More From Your Bible*. Unfortunately, most of them failed that short and simple test. This convinced me more than ever to ground our young people in God's word, and teach them how to relate it to their world. Our youth were theologically challenged as well, so I sought to teach them basic doctrine.

Two things that helped me in my teaching. First, I was tasked by my publisher to write Bible study materials for youth. Before having them published, I taught them to my young people first. Second, our church launched a discipleship program that had us dig into the Word, starting from the basics and gradually moving on.

To be effective in teaching youth, we need to be relational, authentic, interactive, open, and creative. We can't take things for granted, either. It is important to tell the HOW, not just the WHAT and WHY. And, beyond just telling, we need to show them a good example through our own life. Most of all, we should emulate our Master Teacher, Jesus Christ!

7. Pastoral care of young people

I always tell my youth ministry students that if they don't have a heart for young people or feel called to youth work, they have no business to be ministering with the youth. Some Bible school interns or new graduates and young pastors think that youth ministry is easy: just some fun, games, sports and camps. And so they rush into it with misguided expectations. Soon they realize that youth ministry is a lot of hard work, because we are not dealing with robots. We minister to real people who have the ability to think and feel, young lives that are impressionable and in the process of developing into independent individuals. We operate, not merely in the realm of the temporal, but with eternity in mind.

Caring for those younger than myself comes naturally for me as the eldest in the family. When it comes to ministering to the youth, the 'Ate' (older sister) in me is sensitive to the needs of others and seeks to meet those needs, whether it is lending a listening ear to a young person whose love has not been returned; speaking an encouraging or affirming word to one who has just accomplished something, no matter how small it may be; befriending a lonely youth avoided or ostracized by peers; or just giving a hug to someone who looks like s/he needs it.

Thankfully, God paired me with a husband who shares my passion for helping others. He's not only a pastor himself, he's also a counsellor. Through the years, we've been privileged to act as spiritual parents: guiding, training and discipling young people in every aspect of their lives. Some of them literally lived with us in our home. Once, one of them was turned away from his dorm and even the hospital because he had a communicable disease. Although we had a toddler at that time, we welcomed him into our home as he was treated and recovered from his illness.

People before task

While studying at seminary, we learned that we need to be incarnational and relational. I was tested once when, after a meeting with the core youth group, I had to rush home to study for my midterm exams (in youth ministry!). But the young people wanted to hang out and eat together. They kept tugging me towards the nearest mall. Finally, I gave in to what I thought would be a waste of precious time...and actually enjoyed that spontaneous and informal time with them. When we said our goodbyes after a couple of hours, one of them said: "You're really incarnational!". He knew I was going beyond my job description and appreciated what I did.

Sometimes, it's during those casual times that real issues and concerns are shared. In our context, I find that sharing a meal or snack together helps youth relax and open up. I'm also surprised when young people who hardly make eye contact suddenly want to share a problem through SMS or Facebook. Perhaps these digital natives feel more comfortable confiding through cyberspace.

Counseling is not my forte, but when one young man's voice on the other end of the phone said: "I'm holding a knife...give me one good reason why I should not slit my wrist right now!", I calmly made a deal with him: "Can you come and sleep over at our house tonight? We'll talk there. Until then, promise me you'll not hurt yourself". He came over that night, looking his usual jolly self, while he ate dinner with my family and made small talk. I was just waiting for him to start talking about his problem, but he never did. I guess the fact that we cared for him was reason enough to abandon his plan.

8. Working with schools

Being 'the only Christian nation in Asia' has its perks. Our Department of Education has issued an order to 'encourage and promote the teaching of religion to children in public elementary and high schools...'. Therefore, unlike its Asian counterparts, many Philippine schools welcome youth workers who offer Religious Instruction or Moral Values Education. Opportunities to minister in schools are as various as they are numerous. Filipino youth workers serve as school chaplains; religious instructors; sports, music, and performing arts coaches; and values education teachers in public and private schools.

Many groups in our country are involved in campus ministries. Parachurch organizations have been ministering in schools, starting with Inter-Varsity Christian Fellowship (IVCF) in the 50's, then Campus Crusade for Christ (CCC) - now known as Cru - in the mid-60's, and Navigators in the early 70's. They used to work independently, but started working together under the Youth Ministries Executives Network (YMEN) in the late 90's.

There are also denominational student ministries like PSALM (Philippine Student Alliance Lay Movement, which was founded by the Christian and Missionary Alliance Churches of the Philippines in the 60's) and ENCampusPHL (Every Nation Campus of Victory, Philippines, which began in the early 80's). Local churches host student centers, either at their church buildings or rented facilities near schools. Besides discipleship and leadership training, these churches offer students the use of computers, sports equipment and facilities, college entrance exam reviews, camps and retreats, and the like.

My experience

Ever since I was a high school student I have had the chance to minister in schools. I went to a private Roman Catholic school that fielded its senior high school students as religious instructors to nearby public schools. Being a Protestant, I was assigned to non-Catholic students: Protestant and Muslim kids. Now as an adult youth minister I am often invited to speak in schools and handle their retreats for 6th graders up to senior high school students, either on my own, with my husband, or with my youth ministry students from the seminary.

Because I believe it is important to reach not only the youth, but also the significant adults in their lives (i.e. parents, teachers), I have accepted invitations to speak at Parent-Teacher Association meetings, as well as conventions and training for teachers and administrators. Being a writer for Values Education textbooks and magazines for preschool up to high school has, likewise, been my passport into schools via the printed page.

My advice to youth workers in the Philippines

Look beyond your 'borders' and reach your community through schools. The youth you reach now will be tomorrow's leaders of your community, and even our nation. There are SO many schools and not enough campus ministers. (Some public high schools' populations are in the thousands.) There is NO NEED to fight over territory. The best thing is to work together in cooperation, not competition. After all, we have the same Master: Jesus Christ; and the same goal: win the youth for Him.

My advice to all youth workers

Use your God-given talents/gifts to bless, not only your church, but your community as well through the schools.

9. Leading a team and developing others

As a typical Baby Boomer, an eldest child, and growing up in the U.S., I have a distinctive independent streak in me. Thus, it took a while for me to adjust to the idea of working with a team and developing others around me. The process requires intentional effort, and after a couple of decades I am still learning. Though by no means exhaustive, here are seven things I learned about leading a team and developing others around me:

L – Let God lead. God will be God, so let Him be God. It sounds simple and basic enough, but we often forget and rely on our own resources... especially when we feel we are so smart, equipped and gifted. We need to remember that youth ministry is HIS work, and we are His instruments to be this generation's ministers, discipling them to become like Him.

E – Example, example, example. And because we are God's instruments, we are also to be "examples in speech, life and purity." Someone once said it was 'life transference'. Alex Sibley calls it 'life-on-life modeling'.

A – Allow them to fail. If you're a perfectionist like me, you can't help but be frustrated when the leaders you are developing do not succeed in a given task. The tendency is to take over. Don't! Let them learn from their mistakes. It is a better lesson than having you come to the rescue each time they flop.

D – Discover and develop their gifts and talents. One beautiful thing with having a team is that we are bringing in different people with a variety of personalities and abilities. All kinds of people are needed to do youth work. It is not just for the extroverts, jocks, and musicians. Help the leaders discover their unique spiritual gifts and talents. Find ways to equip them so that they can further improve on these. Then empower them for their specific tasks.

E – Expect the best from them. Nothing encourages your leaders more than knowing that you believe in them. They may feel inadequate or lack confidence, but with your prodding, they can do great things for God through the youth ministry.

R – "Rest from your labors." Know when to stop...when to let go. Often, we are like 'helicopter parents' who keep hovering over our youth leaders. After we have developed them and deployed them for their respective duties, we micromanage. Rather, trust that they will accomplish what God has planned for them to do. There comes a time when we need to cut the umbilical cord and release them. And yes, maybe they will even take over where we have left off. That's when we may discover that we have trained them well.

S – Stop being insecure. Let's not fall into the comparison trap, especially when we find that our youth leaders have become 'greater' than us. Instead, let us praise God that He has seen fit to use us to help them develop. And let's not fret when they start relying on other mentors. We can only give so much. Just as *we* have learned from more than one person to develop in different areas of our lives, they too, need different people to help mold them into the person God wants them to be.

10. Parents

Dan Jessen, our first youth ministry professor, used to say: "In youth ministry, you only work one-third of the time with youth. One-third is with adult volunteers, and the other one-third is with parents". Back in the late nineties, the idea of Mark De Vries's *Family-Based Youth Ministry* was a novel idea for us. But it made sense, especially since Filipinos are quite relational and family-oriented. There is a delicate balance to strike, however, as we deal with parents. On the one hand, it is important to establish a relationship with them that is based on transparency, communication, and a mutual love for their kids. We earn parents' trust when we are open, share our plans and dreams for the youth ministry, and keep them updated on the progress of the ministry. We earn their respect when we keep our word, adhere to church policies and reinforce their family's house rules. We earn their love when we sincerely demonstrate care and attention to their children's holistic needs.

On the other hand, we need to be careful that we are not seeking to take the place of parents in the young person's life. There is a great danger of falling into the trap of competing for the young person's time, energy, and even affections. We may feel flattered when they come to us for help and advice, maybe even expressing that we are "the only one" who can understand or relate to them. There are even horror stories of youth workers who have unduly given their young people dilemmas: making them choose between family and 'the Lord's work' and irresponsibly misusing passages such as Luke 14:26. Some go so far as to issue mild threats such as, "Remember, only what's done for Christ will last. Everything else on earth, including your family, is temporal". When one of my youth leaders confided that his mother was becoming jealous of me, warning lights started flashing. I had to check my actions and motives to see if I was intentionally (or even unintentionally) engaged in a parental tug-of-war.

The youth pastor as a bridge

We want the youth to love us, to be close to us. But more than that, we want to bridge the generation, cultural and communication gaps between parents and young people. As partners with parents, I've sought to assist parents by conducting seminars on 'Understanding Youth', starting with Generation X in the nineties, then Generation Y, and now Generation Z and Alpha Generation. During one such seminar, one of the parents commented: "Okay, so now we understand them. But shouldn't understanding and communication work both ways? Why aren't there seminars on 'Understanding Parents'? Do we have to do all the understanding just because we are adults?". Taking her cue, I started conducting workshops on 'Understanding Parents' for the youth as well. My husband, a marriage and family therapist, and I likewise hold family workshops where we seek to bring parents and young people together to teach them about mutual love and understanding.

11. You and senior church leaders

Many problems arise in youth ministry due to communication, whether it's miscommunication or no communication at all. For example, we may assume that our senior leader knows our intention, that we and the leadership team are on the same wavelength, that volunteers know what is expected of them, or that the youth comprehend what we are trying to convey.

My brother, who was a pilot and adopted check lists even in his everyday life, often said: "Never assume anything". When something important is not communicated, we could end up with less than ideal results. Even if it seems basic, obvious, repetitious...it may not be, so communicate it clearly: share your vision and goals with your senior leader, tell your leadership team your plans, inform volunteers of your expectations, ensure that the youth understand exactly what you're saying.

Collaborate

Gone are the days of the one-man-band or Lone Ranger, whether in the corporate world or in ministry. In his book *The Millennium Matrix*, Rex Miller talks about a shift from dominant leaders who operate from the top down to leaders who come alongside their people to work with them. We need to adopt a stance of connecting rather than commanding, cooperating rather than clashing. We need to see others as those who work WITH us and not FOR us.

Baby Boomer youth ministers like myself have had to navigate this difficult change from working on our own to working with a team. But for the younger generation of youth workers, this style of leadership will come more naturally.

Capitulate

Few people enjoy the prospect of giving in, giving way or giving up, especially when it comes to long-held opinions, accustomed methods, laid-out plans, and ideal standards. But in youth ministry (as in any ministry or relationship) there needs to be some give and take. We may think we know what is best for the youth ministry, but perhaps our senior leader, who is more experienced, has a better idea. A member of the leadership team may suggest a new approach that we haven't considered. Don't let pride get in the way of a growing and fruitful ministry. Know when to yield for the sake of God's kingdom.

When all is said and done, submission to God's will and plan for our lives and ministry is of utmost importance.

Chapter 4
Fraser Keay from Scotland

1. My background and how I got into youth ministry

I come from Scotland, which is still part of the U.K., and most of my extended family live there. The scenery in places is stark but beautiful, and as with other countries in Europe we have lots of ancient castles. We Scots have a reputation of being stubborn; we don't tend to give up easily! Part of this is perhaps due to having fought off, successfully at times, Roman as well as English armies. Most Scottish people speak English (not Gaelic) but we have a very strong sense of Scottish identity and a dry 'deadpan' sense of humour. Most men only wear a kilt (a traditional 'skirt' for men) on special occasions such as weddings.

I did not attend church much as a child or teenager, but an older brother did and took me to one once. It made no impact on me and I threw myself into golf, being with friends and drinking. That all changed during my first year as a student in Edinburgh. My room-mate randomly gave me a leaflet about the Christian faith, given to him by a stranger on the street. I read it, and over the next six months became increasingly aware of the presence of God, my own sin and guilt, and the uncertainty of my own eternal destiny. I didn't understand what was happening to me. During a job interview, a Christian man I'd never met before shared the gospel with me. The following Sunday I went along to the same church my brother had taken me to years before. This time I responded. Four weeks later I was led to Christ by another student and powerfully filled with the Holy Spirit immediately afterwards and spoke in tongues. The church was Baptist with a strong emphasis on preaching and mission; many people like me were saved, baptised and filled with the Holy Spirit.

The church and its ministry to students and young workers impacted me a lot. There was a girl there and we became involved in a lot of the same things together - youth work, worship ministry, and it turned out she was going to be studying the same course as me at university. I had previously resolved that I should avoid a relationship during the first two years as a Christian, but I decided that this wonderful and stable girl was too good to miss! She soon became my girlfriend and then, in 1991, my wife. After University I served as a police officer, but my real passion was serving the college student group at church that Anna and I had been asked to lead. In my late 20's I found myself at a crossroads. I never dreamt of working with teenagers full time, but when someone I respected asked what I *really* wanted to do with my life, the penny dropped. God was at work in my heart and within a year we had moved as a family to the other side of the country where I took up a three year post as a church youth worker. At this point we had a two year old and were expecting our second child.

During those three years I realised I needed to better understand theology, as well as youth and family ministry. God led us to Denver Seminary, Colorado, U.S.A., where I could study all three as part of a Master's Degree in Divinity. God also graciously opened a door for me to serve as a part-time youth pastor in a church in Aurora, Colorado. My wife and I, and our two children, stayed there for four years. The Lord provided wonderfully and quite miraculously for my family and me during the entire period.

With a clearer sense of my theology and convictions, we moved to Cardiff, Wales, U.K., where God opened a door for me to serve in a church as a full time youth pastor. I was there for nine years and during that time my role slowly expanded until I became part of the overall leadership of the church, overseeing youth ministry, kids to college ministry leaders, and most things to do with training and discipleship. My wife and I recently moved back to Scotland and I am currently writing two books whilst I work during the day. This book is one of the books. Our children are now adults at university; by the time you read this one of them will just have been married!

2. Looking after your own soul

I have served as a volunteer leader with considerable responsibility, and as a paid youth pastor. If you work in a regular day job you generally work around a given structure. In vocational ministry you have to create your own structure, develop your own rhythm. It is a big adjustment and as one pastor counselled me before I began my first full time role, "You will collect your own assortment of scars". He was right. I have found three things helpful through the years: knowing yourself; having variety; and having friends.

Knowing yourself

One key for me has been getting to know how I best work and to then be disciplined in that. In vocational ministry do I use mornings or lunchtime to spend time with people, or study and pray? Which day should I take as a 'Sabbath' day? (Sunday may not be best). What do I do on my day off since my friends are probably at work? Which mornings or afternoons will I take off? What helps me relax? You can end up working all the time if you don't get to know yourself and develop some sort of structure.

Variety

We sometimes need a little variety to help us regain our focus on Christ. Since our praying and interaction with Scripture are linked, I sometimes move from reading to studying to meditating to memorising Scripture. I listen to the Bible online. You can mix it up. Be creative. Often I have found a specific place and time to pray in the houses we have lived in. If you have young children, sometimes the bathroom is the only place left in the house where you can be alone, so I sometimes went for a walk. Jesus not only got up early to get peace to pray, he once fell asleep in a boat because he was so tired. Sometimes taking a nap can be the most spiritual thing you can do, just maybe not during a Sunday meeting! I love coffee shops where I can think, read and sometimes write out what I am praying or thinking. I have found the writings of Henri Nouwen and Eugene Peterson especially helpful.

Friends

Apart from my wife, several types of friend have been important to me and have helped keep my soul fresh:

1. An accountability partner who regularly asks me tough personal questions (I do the same for him).
2. Friends my own age (especially if you have moved around a lot).
3. Other youth workers to regularly share stories, resources, joys and problems with.
4. Older Christians who will love and support me. I have been particularly helped by an older man who is good at counselling and

supporting leaders.

5. Younger leaders who help you stay sharp (as well as give you a headache sometimes - but, then again, that often drives you back to God!)

3. Singleness, marriage and children

As with most Western countries, in my country it is normal to ask a woman to become your girlfriend when you realise she likes you as well. Parents do not, as a rule, determine who their children marry (although they may use other methods to encourage or discourage the relationship!). It is also normal for a man to ask the parents, sometimes just the father, for permission to marry their daughter. But this is more of a tradition than essential and is because most people in our society simply start to live with each other as if they are married. Some do not get married at all. This is not true of young Christian couples who are committed to Christ and serious about each other, who wait until they are married to live together.

When I became a Christian at 19, girls were a big distraction for me so I promised myself that I would not have a girlfriend, even a Christian girlfriend, for two more years. But God had other ideas and a few months later I met Anna. I soon got to know her parents and family well. It is important to know someone in the context of family. There have been several things important to us with marriage, family and children: prayer and advice; partnership and hospitality.

Prayer and advice

An older leader at church taught us how to conduct ourselves as young Christian couples. As I did not have a Christian background I needed all the advice I could get. My love for Anna grew and 18 months later I asked her to marry me. I remember fasting and praying first to see if this was God's will. We did not have much money since we were still students, so we prayed about this too and God provided wonderfully for us.

If you want to build something enduring you have to plan thoroughly before you start. Before we got married, we prepared for it. Getting prepared for marriage by learning from an older married couple is a great way to learn, even if our parents have given us an excellent example.

We met with an older married couple to talk and we have done this for younger couples since then. Our first few years of marriage showed me how selfish I could be, so I met with an older godly man for advice and prayer. We have been married now for almost 25 years and are very much a team, and complement each other's skills.

Prayer and partnership

Married youth pastors are in a good position to demonstrate a stable marriage to young people. But do not kill your marriage or hurt your children because of work or youth ministry. You do not marry a youth ministry, you marry a spouse.

Whilst in youth ministry, we prayed together most nights about people and things that mattered to us, not just young people. We opened up our home to students and young people, whom we simply loved having round. When we bought our first house we prayerfully chose somewhere which could be easily reached by the young people. Many times we have had important conversations with young people in our home, while they helped us wash up dishes after a meeting, or when driving them home in a car or minibus. Some of them would linger behind, a sure indication that they wanted to talk.

Children

We always involved our two young children in what we did, but without sacrificing them on the altar of ministry, which is easy to do if you are busy. One of our children took her very first steps in front of a room full of young people. Our children have different personalities, though both have a great sense of humour. One child has gone on to be a volunteer youth leader herself and the other contributes more behind-the-scenes, e.g. developing the website and cover for this book. When our children were in the youth ministry I made sure that they had other leaders (not me) in charge of their particular group. When they got to age 14, I also agreed with them that I would not go into their school year as a youth worker - otherwise I would be in youth group, in church, at home, almost everywhere they were! Sometimes at a summer camp I would hardly see them all week until we came home. That's OK. We are a close family, but as they grow older children need their own space to develop socially whilst still appreciating their parents and seeing them as trusted friends and advisors.

As a family we have lived in three different countries doing youth ministry. One important piece of advice we got was, "Move when your children move". If your children are at school, if at all possible, try to move when they do, e.g. when they move into primary (elementary) school, secondary (high) school, or go to college. We did this twice and believe it reduced some of the impact of a major family transition. Discerning God's call on your life includes discerning the needs of your own family; it is not separate to that call.

4. Organising yourself and your ministry

I started youth ministry as someone who is naturally quite organised, especially with things I am passionate about; but at times I have needed help to organise things. After all, pastors are not there primarily to organise! My wife is a superb organiser and church secretaries, along with many parents, have been very helpful. As my ministry in my last church widened I was fortunate to have on my team two female volunteer leaders who not only cared for the young people but were able to organise what I did not have time to organise. But, in my experience, most young youth workers are disorganised, especially young men. Some are tempted to think they don't even need to be organised but just need to 'hang out' with the young people. This is naive, frustrating for other volunteers, and it does not help build a team. So here is my advice.

If you are disorganised

Admit it and find someone who is organised. If everyone on your team is disorganised then ask someone who *is* organised to join your team in an administrative role. People often just need to be asked to help. Get them to show *you* how to organise. Delegate. God has gifted others with administrative abilities for a reason - to help the church, including the youth ministry, to grow (1 Cor 12:28)! Be encouraged; you *will* grow in this area of life and ministry and will develop your own methods.

My father also gave me a good piece of advice: "Touch everything once". What he meant was that if you are dealing with emails, paperwork, or phone calls try to complete them in one sitting, otherwise you can actually end up handling them many times, and so waste time procrastinating.

Determine where you are going and specifically how you are going to get there

Where you are going should be driven by what you value. Add your values together and you have a 'philosophy of ministry'. It might be just five simple things. For example, if one core value is 'Team Work', then one key goal resulting from that might be 'Recruit more leaders'. So how *specifically* are you going to do that? 'Recruit more leaders *by speaking to people between March and May each year*'. I realised that waiting until summer to recruit more leaders was normally too late because youth activities began in September. I also spoke to existing leaders during that same three month period to review their year with them and see if they wanted to commit to another year from September. Another value might be 'Present Christ to young people'. A related goal might be 'Hold an annual winter camp to impact young people for Christ'. Be specific in your planning. Be sure to have a backup plan. What if the person in charge of cooking gets sick the day before you all leave? What if the weather turns really bad? This is all part of organising. The best book I have read on organising a youth programme is Jonathan McKee's 'The Top 12 Resources Youth Workers Want'. Remember, involve people who are more organised than you, and delegate!

5. Keeping your evangelism edge sharp

If the leadership of your church is evangelistic it helps your youth ministry grow. It is no surprise that large youth ministries are usually found in large churches. The one exception I know was a church with a youth group four times larger than the church itself! The youth leader was a great evangelist and soon moved into evangelism full time. If a church is more interested in maintaining their traditions, or the leadership has significant problems, then the whole church - including the youth work - will struggle in this area. I have experienced both helpful and difficult situations. Remember, youth ministry is not done in a vacuum. Determining whether your strategy will be from 'in to out' (starting with the teenagers already in the church), or from 'out to in' (starting with a group who have nothing to do with the church) is also wise.

Friendship

In all my years of youth ministry, the most effective way I have seen evangelism work is through friendship. We read that Andrew brought Peter to Jesus (John 1:41-42). A young person who is good friends with someone will be praying for them and ask them to come to youth group, a retreat or Sunday church meeting. It is no different than with children or adults. God usually uses the believer to bring that person to Jesus. Encourage this. Remember that young people differ in their friendship circles. Some have few friends, but deeper friendships. Some have gazillions of friends and can bring them all to a youth group or meeting at the drop of a hat. Both are valuable.

With that backdrop, here are a few methods I have used over the last twenty-five years to train young people and college students in evangelism. There are lots of others. Do what God puts in your heart and stick to it. A clear method is better than no method! In all these the Holy Spirit is central, because without Him our methods are just empty.

Course evangelism

Courses like the 'Alpha Course' or 'Christianity Explored' are where young people bring their friends to a relaxed and fun environment where they are free to ask questions after food and good short talk or video. People are free to openly agree or disagree in their small group afterwards about what the speaker has said. This method of evangelism also includes a wide variety of people: cooks, hosts, people who pray and people who help answer questions.

Preaching and teaching evangelism

This may be at a weekly youth service, camp or in a main church meeting or special church service. Use the people most gifted in explaining the faith and bringing young people to faith; that might be a young person. You will learn which preachers the youth enjoy (and don't). Ask young people to share their testimony; personal stories are important.

Young people brought up in Christian homes also need to know God for themselves. It does not happen automatically. Their parents can help them see Christ; so can the youth team. Do not teach them mere moral lessons - 'how to' or 'be this' or 'be that' - or they will think the Christian life is all about rules or 'being a good person'. Point to Jesus through Old Testament stories, the law, prophecies, Psalms, Gospels, epistles, etc. Scripture makes us wise for salvation, and that is found in Christ, not 'being good'.

Literature and social media evangelism

I have given timid young people gospel leaflets to encourage them to start sharing the gospel by handing them to a friend. My own faith journey started because a young person handed me a booklet and I started reading it. Social media also works by way of helpful blogs, chat rooms, videos, etc, that people can be directed to or help develop.

Personal evangelism

Some people are *particularly* good at this; they are better than most at explaining the gospel clearly and relevantly using everyday language and capitalising on everyday situations and conversations. They also sense when someone is ready to decide to become a Christian. It may be as simple as asking at the right time, 'Is there anything stopping you becoming a Christian?'. Help train your young people in how to explain the gospel simply in a few easy steps using an object or a story.

Prophetic evangelism

Sometimes called 'Treasure Hunting' (see Kevin Dedmon's book) is when small teams of young people with an adult leader pray together for words of knowledge from God before setting off into a town or busy place to find the particular people God wants them to find. Many believers find it nerve-wracking but incredibly faith-building as God opens up the way to pray for someone for physical healing, or for healing about a difficult situation (hey, didn't Jesus do that?).

6. Communicating with youth

When I started working with young people I reckoned that if the main preacher in church did the 'A, B, C' of the gospel, then it was my job to teach the young people the 'P, Q and R', i.e. those things the young people would find *particularly* helpful at their stage in life. I then developed that, and tried to address three key questions in making a three year teaching plan; one for 11-14 year olds and one for 14-17 year olds. The questions were:

1. What do they need to know? (knowing)
2. How will it shape their character? (being)
3. What difference will it make to their lives practically? (doing)

I did not become a slave to the plan but used it as an outline. I made sure church parents knew about it. If a young person has Christian parents then *they* are the main disciplers along with rest of the church, not the youth pastor and team. The outline also helped stop me teaching only my favourite subjects and made sure the young people got a balanced Bible diet. I also synchronised it with the main Sunday preaching plan so they complemented each other.

Effective interpretation

One key 'interpretation question' I use is, "What does the Bible passage says about God's *Messiah* and God's *Mission*, i.e. 'Jesus and the Kingdom of God"? You find this theme at the start and end of the book of Acts. This helps point people to Jesus and avoids an emphasis on 'be good' or 'be better' which deprives young people of an understanding of God's enabling grace and the gospel. I study the Bible passage or topic and teach *one* main point they will remember, in a creative way they will remember.

Effective methods

In my early days I used to think young people should just listen to me preach. I then studied the gospels and realised Jesus used a variety of teaching methods, such as small group discussion, sending the disciples on trips, asking them questions, spending lots of time with them, tasking them with things, making a point when something important happened suddenly in front of them all, time away together, using stories or everyday objects familiar to them, doing good deeds, praying for healing, and using prophetic words. Alongside his preaching, Jesus' teaching method was actually one long mission with training on the job for his disciples. It is also very important to understand (youth) culture where you are. Just as Paul used everyday things familiar to those in Athens (Acts 17), so we should do the same so that our communication is relevant to our young listeners, not just 'theologically correct'. I developed and often taught a half-day seminar called 'Jesus and Learning Styles' to help other leaders understand that a variety of methods are important to reach every young person.

You, however, are not necessarily the sole source of teaching. Sometimes I ask others to help with creative ideas as I can run out of them. Usually, the madder the ideas the better! I also have guest speakers and people sharing their testimony, which is particularly effective if it reveals a side to the church member that the youth know nothing about.

7. Pastoral care of young people

I used to think that 'pastoral care' meant sitting with old people having a cup of tea or coffee. But I learned from two pastors skilled in this area. I made sure that I had money set aside for spending time with young people, leaders, and parents of young people. I would split my pastoral care time equally between the three. I sometimes gave others on the team 'pastoral expenses money' to use to buy drinks for themselves and the young people they were talking with at cafes, etc. Good pastors do this; so should youth pastors.

My wife is good at spotting people's needs so she encourages me to invite certain young people, or leaders, for dinner. Having people to your house is important, because leadership includes showing hospitality. More than once we have had young people stay overnight with us because a crisis in their family meant it was better for them stay away from the home for a while.

Human development

One of my youth ministry professors Larry Lindquist used the following illustration to remind us that adolescents are growing in *five* main ways. As a conductor (Larry is also a musician) firmly holds a baton in his hand, a rounded pastor and youth ministry will have a firm 'grip' and cover, on a weekly basis, all five of these areas that young people are developing in:

1. The thumb is the most physical (strongest) digit on your hand. Attend to *physical* growth and needs: younger youth especially need to be active.
2. Put your forefinger on the side of your head. Inside is your brain. Attend to *intellectual* growth and needs: make young people think.
3. In some cultures if you stick up your middle finger at someone it is offensive. Attend to *moral* and *spiritual* needs: challenge the heart.
4. Your fourth finger is often the weakest and, like it, our emotions are often the weakest part of us. Attend to *emotional* needs: support young people and help them learn to support each other, and in whatever family matters you are aware of.
5. I have a good friend whose smallest finger curls up when he drinks tea with friends. Attend to *social* needs: allow plenty time to relax and have fun!

Remember gender differences

In general, girls talk face to face whilst boys talk side by side *doing* something together (same with most men). You also just don't know when a young person might want to talk. I once helped a 13 year old boy with some issues while we threw a frisbee across his back garden for half an hour. Encourage your team to care face to face or side to side with young people, depending on the young person. If a young person initiates a hug then side to side is preferable.

Pastoral care should be proactive

Pastoral care involves advance planning. For weekends away and camps we divided the young people between leaders so they were properly cared for. In big groups young people can get lost. It is why having small groups as part of your ministry is wise, either on their own or as one element in a youth group meeting. Small groups are common sense which is why most churches have them, often using people's homes (Acts 2:46). They do not have to be on an evening at 7.30pm.

Sometimes it is important to wait for someone to come to us as it can show they truly want to be helped. But Jesus did not always wait for people to come to him, e.g. he went to Zaccheus's house, and other people's houses. He called and trained new leaders. The parable of the lost sheep, and the prophet Ezekiel (chapter 34) show us that good shepherds *pursue* straying and lost sheep as well as helping heal broken and bruised ones. I have set up mentoring programmes, taught in church, and led seminars to enccurage mentoring across the church because by creating a strong mentoring culture the 'load' of pastoral care is spread out and many pastoral issues are identified and dealt with at an earlier stage. Of course this is not the primary purpose of mentoring but it is a good secondary benefit.

Their safety and yours

Avoid succumbing to the 'Little Messiah' trap where you think you are the only person who can solve a young person's problems, or the young person is led to believe the youth pastor is the *only* one understands them. It is a trap some lead pastors fall into when counselling adults; some end up having an affair with the person they are counselling. Along with unforgiveness, thinking you are indispensable is the sin of pride and a common strategy of the enemy Satan to destroy lives and ministries. Avoid both!

A good maxim is, 'If in doubt, refer'. This could involve keeping a list of resources or people available, e.g. rape crisis centre telephone number, bullying help-line, and a doctor in a church to call if you have a question.

In general, youth workers should never be alone with a young person. The only time I did this was if they wanted to tell me something very important and wanted to be alone for a moment to tell me. It was usually in a side room with the door open, or at a cafe where everyone there could see us, but not hear us, or with my wife at our home. Your church should have a clear written policy that deals with this and other aspects of working with young people and children; make sure you know it well. A church with a good, caring reputation brings glory to God and blesses the community it serves.

Communication with church leaders and parents

If you learn that a young person from a church family has major problems, then first ask trusted church leaders if they know anything. There may be marriage, family or other problems you are not aware of; it may alert the church leaders to a problem *they* were not aware of. I once counselled a teenage boy who had stolen some items and was arrested by the police. It turned out he was actually worried about his parent's marriage, so he did something crazy to get them talking properly! It opened the door for the parents to receive marriage counselling.

8. Working with schools

Dean Borgman, an American youth ministry veteran in his 80's, whom I had the chance to meet, argues in his book *Hear My Story* that the five key shapers that influence young people growing up are: parents, peers, media, church and the school/community. We, the Church, need to serve and 'shape the shapers' where we can. Schools certainly shape young people.

The United Kingdom

At present all schools in the U.K. must provide for the spiritual and moral welfare of pupils; this includes teaching on religion with an emphasis on the Christian faith. But with greater secularism this is harder to implement practically. Religious education can be more about ethics and any act of worship at a school assembly may be more like a school news bulletin. In any case, it is wrong to force individuals to worship. However, the opportunity is still there for Christians who are school teachers, pastors, and youth workers to have good relationships with senior school teachers and use their skills to serve the school by helping with sport or music, offering pastoral support to pupils, serving on school boards and committees, providing dynamic multimedia presentations (especially at Easter and Christmas), taking religious and sex education classes, and helping older Christian pupils lead prayer and Bible teaching groups at lunchtimes. Some pastors act as the school chaplain.

My experience

The more I matured in youth ministry, the more I saw the value of working with schools. In Denver, USA, I was youth pastor to teenagers who came from *six* different high schools with an almost equal mix of public, private Christian, and home-schooled children (the first few weeks at youth group were very interesting). As I was also studying full time I had less time to access public schools but got into a few (see Gary

McCusker's section on this regarding the USA). In Wales I worked with the local high school helping with sport, social education, religious education classes and the school Christian Union. It is helpful for church youth to see their youth pastor and other youth volunteers there, even if some of them face the dilemma of their church and school 'worlds' colliding and being exposed as 'going to church' by you being there (!).

My advice to other youth workers

1. Make sure your church, and especially church leaders, are properly behind you and fully aware of what you are praying/doing/thinking about the school. This gives information for prayer and better ownership from the church.
2. In liaison with church leaders, ask for a parent in your church to partner with a parent from another church, and form a regular prayer group to pray for school/s in your area.
3. Go slow and build genuine trust with key staff and teachers. Like a strong tree trust takes time to grow, and can be cut down in just 2 minutes if you or someone else says or does something stupid. A great website for UK youth workers is www.schoolswork.co.uk.
4. View yourself as a servant to the school; after all, you are on *their* turf.

9. Leading a team and developing others

My experience over the last thirty years of leading, and being led, includes various jobs and being part of three church staff teams. In my last ministry position I implemented a youth worker apprenticeship programme that over eight years drew twelve people from four different countries.

Proper shepherding takes a team. Jesus appointed twelve and Peter was first (Luke 6:12), but among equals. Paul and Barnabas *always* appointed eldership teams, not one man. Youth ministry should reflect this sort of biblical teamwork with the youth pastor or main leader as 'first among equals', a 'lead youth worker among other youth workers' who together with the church leadership determine and set out a God-given vision for the ministry. Along with the rest of the church they reach and care for young people. It takes a village, the whole church, to raise a child! That should encourage us. In my first youth leader role there were just three of us on the team. In another, 44% of the volunteers resigned within three months of my arrival (at first I thought I had bad breath but many were just holding on until a new youth pastor arrived). Regardless of the size of the youth group or any hurdles it is the whole church's responsibility. This will help ensure that young people are integrated into the local church. Overall, here are four things I have learned.

Like Jesus, take time to draw your team together and personally encourage and mentor younger leaders.

Jesus spent many hours with his disciples, both showing them what he did, helping them do it, and then leaving. So include your whole team in the planning process and develop others *as you lead*. Give personal time to help younger leaders and make sure the whole team is heard and the majority OK with decisions you make. Pray, lead meetings well and finish on time. I've also had older teenagers and parents as part of the team, or sitting in to give their input. 16-18 year olds can make great helpers and young leaders for ministry to 11-14 year olds. Teenagers can be superb working with much younger children. We've read good youth ministry books together (like this one!) and as a team had overnight and weekend retreats together to consider important issues.

Do not ignore younger leaders and do not interfere with more mature leaders; give the right amount of time to each depending on their life and (youth) ministry experience.

In one of my first jobs as a trainee the manager completely ignored me for most of the time. Later, I took a lot of his leadership style and turned it upside down - I now had a good model of how to help younger leaders! Another boss I worked for was incompetent and interfering, which was also unhelpful since I was by then very experienced. Neither bosses were easy to work with but I learned a lot. To ensure I am doing OK I sometimes ask younger leaders to give me a mark out of 10 (1 point for terrible and 10 for brilliant) as to how they think I am doing in mentoring them. This gives them the chance to give me feedback using just a number and it allows for further discussion if needed.

Try and have on your team a 'spine' of long-term, mature leaders combined with short-term, younger leaders much closer in age to the young people.

I've had many superb youth leaders, some as young as 15, and some in their 50's who simply needed to be asked onto the team. Some will be with you for a short time because they are young; they are often great catalysts. Others stay on the team for many years and form the backbone of your volunteer team. In one place I served, I asked for a three-year commitment from volunteers; I knew it would stabilise the youth ministry which had suffered under poor and temporary leadership before. Volunteers accepted the challenge as they could see I was not going to suddenly leave. I ended up being the longest serving youth pastor the church ever had. I was recently reminded by the children's ministry leaders in one church that I had asked them to give a seven year commitment. I had forgotten, but it would have been to see an entire cohort of children all the way through the 7 primary school years. They ended up serving for ten!

Plan a volunteer celebration evening for the end of each year. You could ask two parents to help you plan a memorable evening when you can eat, laugh, honour and thank your team. I sometimes did this for all the children's and youth leaders combined. It seemed such a small 'thank you' for their hard work and commitment, but they appreciated it.

People on your team who are a pain in the neck just now may one day end up being a blessing - don't avoid confronting them, but don't give up on them either!

On any team there will be dominant individuals, or those with personal problems that you were not really aware of when you started leading. Some find it hard to respond to a new team leader, especially if you are younger. You need to respect experienced volunteers. Yet some can be quite happy to openly challenge you in your role. Others may try and disrupt things behind the scenes. This can take up a lot of your emotional energy. For the sake of the team, yourself and your ministry you need to deal with it early on. Speak to a pastor or elder in the church about the person and ask if others have found them difficult to work with. I managed to win over most stubborn people. I also realised that the ones I could not gradually win over often did not like *anyone* telling them what to do! Young, talented but maverick leaders are especially difficult to handle, but if you have the skill and can get hold of them they can be very useful in the Kingdom of God. Jesus rebuked the promising but loud-mouth Peter more than the others; he saw his potential but was not 'soft' on him. Like Peter, maverick leaders are often vulnerable inside and often need a firm but kind father in the faith. If you can't be like a father to them help them find one. It may save you and them a lot of unnecessary pain in the long run.

10. Parents

Starting out in youth ministry, especially if you are in your early 20's, can make navigating the parents of teenagers seem like a minefield. You are not sure what to do, or wonder why connecting to them is that important. You may not have long left home yourself! Many of the young people may see you as young, trendy or cool (in contrast to their parents) and may be surprised that you would bother with their parents. For those from Christian homes you may also offer a completely different picture of what a Christian is. The reality, however, is that any young person exploring faith and how it works needs the example of *all* generations in front of them, not just youth leaders and not just older generations separately. The old African proverb, 'It takes a village to raise a child', has a lot of truth to it, and we in Scotland, as with most western countries, have lost a lot of this community dynamic. The main reason I studied theology with youth *and* family ministry at Seminary was to better understand and apply such universal truths. Chap Clark, Marv Penner and Mark DeVries all write well on youth *and* family ministry.

Since it is a family, a local church should be the best place to see different generations interact. Youth ministry has an absolutely vital place in any local church ministry but should not be completely separate from it, any more than teenagers should be completely removed from their own family - unless that family is a threat to their health or life.

Like some of the writers of this book I had my own teenagers in the youth ministry I led, so I can see it from the 'youth pastor' and also the 'parent' point of view. Here are some simple points.

Connect and recruit

You are a partner with parents in the life-building and caring process, and also in the faith-building process if a young person has Christian parents. Start by simply talking to parents of teenagers, e.g. before or after youth group. Some parents don't care and see youth group as merely as a place to drop off their children (some parents may not even know they are there, as their children may have lied to them as to their whereabouts!). You and your team need to do your part well. Make sure you have written permission from parents of young people regularly at your activities. Make sure consent forms are used where needed.

Young people also need to know clearly that you are not taking sides or telling their parents about them, especially at parent meetings. As I grew in experience I engaged with parents more, letting them know the youth ministry plans, and getting their input. Visiting family homes was also important to help build trust and I got to see the teenager in their own home. Jesus went into people's homes, and not just when they were sick.

Ask parents to help in the ministry, e.g. in administration, driving, etc. Some may become regular leaders on the youth team - if their children are OK with it. I always asked the teenager/s concerned first, otherwise it could backfire. Some loved having their parent in youth ministry, as did their friends; they were like 'aunts' or 'uncles'. If you ask the teenagers who they'd like on the youth team you'll be surprised which people come up! If it's a parent, knowing that the young people would love them on the team can persuade them to join.

Encourage and educate

Like you, parents are human. They need encouragement. Tell them how well liked or how helpful their child is, or how you enjoy this or that about having them in the youth ministry. If their child is not so helpful, then address it and find something genuinely positive to say - the good image of God is not completely removed from any young person! Parents also appreciate it if you admit where you have made a mistake.

If you are younger, you can probably help parents to better understand youth culture since you only recently left it and understand it well. For example, you could discuss with parents how you see new mobile/cell phone technology impacting teenagers. I arranged regular gatherings for parents that allowed them to talk about common issues they were facing with their children. A respected older parent partnered with me as a 'parent champion'. I often drew some fathers together to pray for their boys who were wandering away from the faith. All these helped connect, encourage, recruit and educate parents. I learned a lot as a fellow parent too! If you are older, parents tend to find it easier to immediately trust you, simply because you've got more life, experience, and maybe children of your own. Move naturally with your age and life-stage. Don't be someone you're not.

11. You and senior church leaders

Your relationship with a senior leader or leadership does not define you, but it will certainly shape you. It is the same in *any* job or task. I have at times been greatly encouraged, or discouraged, by senior leaders and leadership teams. Here are three important lessons I have learned.

'Chew the fish and spit out the bones', i.e. take the good things from a senior leader or leadership team and throw out the bad

Older pastors, elders and trustees have lots of qualities you can learn from. You can also learn from their weaknesses. Try and understand their strengths, weaknesses, and personality; this will help you better serve alongside them. I have worked with good and also poor team leaders. I have known many young youth pastors and workers struggle with poor leadership and supervision; some never go back into church youth work or ministry because of this. But you can learn from good and bad leadership. If things are great then rejoice! If things are bad then speak with another more experienced youth pastor or an experienced church leader well away from your situation; they can help you get perspective and calmly decide what to do. You could even contact one the contributors of this book for advice. I'm sure they'd be happy to help.

Treat leaders' children the same as other young people

Regardless of your situation, treat any pastor or elders' children the same as the rest of the youth - with impartiality. They may already feel some pressure because of who their father or mother is, and you work closely with their Mum or Dad. Let them be themselves and encourage them.

Make sure your vision for the youth fits inside the umbrella vision of the church and its leadership

Be sure *you* own the vision of the church and its leadership, and that your volunteers are on board too. I have had to turn down potential volunteers because they either did not respect the leadership, wanted to pursue their own agenda with the young people, or were intent on showing favouritism to a few select young people. Youth ministry should be like building a room that is part of a house (the church), but to which young people have direct access, i.e. its own door to the outside. It should not be like a shed in the garden that has little to do with the house. This helps the young people slowly integrate into the body of the church when they come to faith. In his letter to the Ephesians, Paul strongly underlines the fact the church is one body, so its various ministries should form part of it and not be a completely separate enterprise.

Chapter 5

Younus Samuel from India

My chapter is dedicated to my heroes of faith, the late Rev. Earl Stubbs and my current Senior Pastor, Rev. Arlene Stubbs who championed the cause of Youth Ministry in our church. Also to Rev. Valson Varghese, Joseph John and John Victor - the trail blazers of the youth ministry, who inspired me greatly.

1. My background and how I got into youth ministry

I come from a land we love to refer to as 'Incredible' India. We are the world's second most populated country. Nowhere on earth does humanity present itself in such a dizzying, creative burst of cultures and religions, races and tongues. Religion is central to Indian culture, and its practice can be seen in virtually every aspect of life in the country. The dominant faith is Hinduism and less than 5% are Christians. What stands out is the diversity of India due to its large size, because of which it is referred to as a sub-continent. Striving towards unity in diversity keeps the nation together.

I grew up in the city of Hyderabad where my father pastored a church. My father has been a great source of encouragement and influence in my life. Being a very strong believer in the Lord Jesus Christ, my father works as an evangelist and also pastors a Church in Hyderabad. I grew up literally 20 feet from our church, in the parsonage, and it was there I learned about family, church, and ministry. I watched the ministry of my dad grow and numerous lives blessed by his ministry. As a child I observed how my father toiled as a pastor and I secretly vowed I would never be a pastor!

Due to the godly upbringing I had, it didn't take me long to put my faith in Jesus. During my college days I started to attend an Assembly of God church. The Lord brought clarity to my life, and my perspective began to change. I decreased and He increased. It was a turning point in my life.

I worked for the financial company Citigroup for eight years and the Lord blessed me and used me mightily for his work. He enabled me to set a godly example for all those around me. I attended a youth camp in

1996 and this changed it all. My life took on a new refreshing turn. I followed the Lord in the waters of baptism and received the baptism of the Holy Spirit soon after. Three years later, in 1999, I gave my life to God for missions. I've always had a passion to reach out to the young people of my city to mentor and counsel them.

In the very next year, in 2000, God called me to serve as the youth pastor at New Life Assembly of God Church in Hyderabad, India. I had many doubts and questions but I was certain of one thing, that the God who called me was faithful and I needed to obey Him. So I joined the church as the youth pastor and served for more than 10 years. I married the beautiful girl of my dreams, Ujjwala, and God blessed us with two lovely kids, Jonathan and Rhea. They are now aged 10 and 7.

It's been an amazing journey being part of the pastoral team of a pentecostal church which has a congregation of more than 5,000. Since the death of our senior pastor a few years ago, I have been entrusted with more responsibility; it has been a challenging but fulfilling task. I successfully went on to complete my Master's in Divinity and earned the credentials needed for a pastor in my context. Not long ago I handed over my role as the full time youth pastor and moved on to be associate pastor at the church. I consider it an honour to work at my home church as a pastor.

2. Looking after your own soul

If the early days of my Christian life had been drawn as a graph, it would have been up and down like the stock market....three days up and then four days down. But undoubtedly more downs than ups. The youth camp in 1996 changed it all, because I decided to follow the Lord through the waters of baptism and also received the baptism of the Holy Spirit. Since then I developed a real hunger and passion for the Lord.

I did not look back and began to seek the Lord as in Psalm 42: 1, which says, "As the deer pants for the water brooks, so pants my soul for You, O God. My soul thirsts for God, for the living God". My thirst for God made me wake up early at dawn and go to the mountains to spend time with God - reading the Bible and talking to Him. I started maintaining a daily journal to record whatever the Lord would say to me in those times. I would even attend two services on a Sunday morning. My friends would often tease me that if there was a third service...I could speak the message instead of the pastor! I decided to stop watching TV & movies for 10 years so I could spend more time with God. I spent long hours during the summer on my terrace, praising and worshipping God with my guitar. I fasted for 40 days during the seasons of Lent, along with my father. Those were my foundational days which I can never forget; they gave me the right perspective on my walk with God.

One of the first things I did as a youth pastor was to put together a prayer team. The entire core team would fast and pray every Saturday. We would come to church early and pray together, asking God to send revival.

I soon realized that youth ministry is very time consuming. Whenever someone calls and says he or she wants to speak for a few minutes, you can be rest assured it will be an hour before the conversation ends! Over a period of time you realize that ministry has overtaken your time with God; at the end of the day it leaves you feeling very dry. I have learnt to manage time with people more effectively and how to conduct shorter and more focused conversations, thus saving a lot of time. I have also determined not to compromise on my time with God for anything. I have decided that if I have a busy day then it will be my sleep that suffers, not my time with the Lord.

I have experienced times of burn out, when I strived too hard and did not see encouraging results. It was then I realized the great need for the Holy Spirit in all my dealings and ministry. So I spend quality time fasting and praying, seeking God's guidance and presence in every aspect of my ministry. I sometimes take time off to be alone with God for 3-4 days.

As a leader, the first person I need to lead is me. "The first person that I should try to change is me" John C. Maxwell said. So my priority as a youth pastor has always been to walk with Jesus and to lead myself first so I can lead others. As Paul says in 1 Corinthians 9:27 (NIV)..."so that after I have preached to others, I myself will not be disqualified for the prize". I understand that my leadership flows from the depth of my relationship with Christ. It's like inhaling Christ and exhaling ministry.

3. Singleness, marriage and children

Marriage in India is considered a very sacred bond; the utmost care and attention is taken to keep a marriage going. Traditionally, parents found the match for their children and the marriage was formalized strictly as per the traditions of the society. It was termed as 'arranged marriage'. However, with time, people in India have accepted the concept of 'love marriage' (where the choice of partner is made by the couple themselves). Today, at least in a church like ours, about 70 % of marriages are 'love marriages', even though this goes against Indian culture.

Youth ministry before and after marriage

Before I joined the church as a full time pastor in 2000 I worked for Citibank through the week and during my spare time I worked tirelessly in ministry. My tag line was, "Anytime" and the youth would echo – "All the Time!". There was one group of young people who wanted me to devote all my spare time outside of work and another group (in the core team) who always asked me to quit my job and come into full time ministry.

As a bachelor I spent long hours counseling the youth, spending time with them in person, over the phone or in restaurants, going to where they were in order to reach out to them. When I met my wife, Ujjwala she was also part of our youth ministry 'Youth Alive'. After two years of courtship and prayer, I proposed to her and we got married. I soon realized I did not have the kind of time I had earlier. I had responsibilities towards my spouse, and then we had children. I had to make a conscious decision to stop taking calls at unearthly hours! I needed to strike a balance.

Boundary setting became essential. For instance, not taking any calls on my phone while on a vacation made the family feel that they were a priority and gave me a much needed break from ministry too! Learning to say "No" to some tasks which others can do also provided more time for the family. I have made it mandatory, every Monday, to spend exclusive time with my family, which has greatly enriched my family life. Whenever possible I take them on a holiday and pamper them so that they understand that amidst all the busy and hectic schedules they are very important to me.

My advice

If you are unmarried, do as much as possible and all that you can and desire to do. Once you are married you will be able to do probably 50% less. God wants you to have a good marriage and this will undoubtedly change your priorities. As a pastor, 'only ministry' or 'only family' will make us feel guilty. So, where is the balance to be found? I believe, "But as for me and my household, we will serve the Lord" (Joshua 24:15). Involving children in their own way in ministry, especially in children's ministry, is very fulfilling; we are then ministering and working together as a family. I strongly believe that it is very rewarding working alongside my wife, as the Bible says, "Two people are better off than one, for they can help each other succeed'" (New Living Translation).

4. Organising yourself and your ministry

I had a great passion for the youth ministry and so I left no stone unturned to do all I could to be successful. But I was a little disorganized! I never turned down a request to do something, and so many times at the end of the day I realized that I had not done some of the jobs I had promised I would do. Since I freely shared my mobile number with everyone I soon realized that I was easily accessible to everyone. The expectations of me were high. Some of them were unrealistic! I realized I need to sort things out if I was to be more effective.

Youth ministry requires you to do a lot of creative things and regularly surprises you. You need to balance entertainment and serious Bible teaching. I found this daunting. The ministry was growing in numbers. My passion to excel for the Lord was also increasing. One thing I found that paid great dividends was planning an annual calendar of youth events. Every event for every month was planned and in place for an entire calendar year. This meant I could begin to execute tasks more effectively.

As the youth pastor I realized that when young people are given responsibility they excel and come out with great ideas. Co-ordinating and giving credit to them for their initiatives, while not being harsh on any failures, helped me create a band of faithful volunteers who would give their life to keep the ministry growing. The ministry started to grow qualitatively as more people joined in and put their time and talents toward the same goal.

Youth Alive, as our youth group was called, became a household name with 22 departments in operation. They effectively planned the events and shouldered the responsibility of executing them, be it the prayer department, choreography department, games and activities department, outreach department, or the mission trips department, etc.

We met every Saturday evening for our fellowship. The Saturdays were also classified as Regular Saturday nights, Odd Saturdays and Special Saturdays, when special events were held. The worship time became awesome and soul lifting, there was effective prayer ministry, the interests of the ever-wandering mind of the youth were captured and the numbers started to swell. According to the biblical command, "Remember your creator in the days of your youth" (Ecclesiastes 12:1), every Saturday we saw people thirsting for God, running to the altar and committing their lives to Christ; there was now a great passion to win souls.

My advice to every aspiring youth worker is to this:

- Match your enthusiasm with commitment.
- As the ministry grows learn to delegate your responsibility; you will be more effective.
- Learn to identify and prepare new leaders so that you have confidence and support in all your endeavors; this helps you keep on target.
- Learn to foresee the growth of your ministry and so plan and set goals so that you are not found lacking or staggering.

5. Keeping your evangelism edge sharp

Evangelism has been a forté of the Youth Alive ministry of our church. I believe the key to effectiveness in this direction is prayer. The prayer movement that began with just ten youth leaders had a tremendous impact on the ministry. There was a great revival among the youth we were ministering to and they developed a hunger and thirst for evangelism.

The vision of the youth ministry is to be mission oriented, aim for growth, establish leadership and provide training. This vision is implanted in the youth leadership at the beginning of each New Year in the month of January. The entire team is taken on a day out and the calendar of the events for the entire year is presented to them so that it is imprinted in their minds and we begin to pray and plan towards it. The yearly calendar is divided broadly into Regular and Odd Saturday nights. Different programmes are scheduled for each. For example, Regular Saturday nights include praise & worship, sharing a testimony and a special welcome to the newcomers. Odd Saturday nights include potluck evening where everyone brings some food to share, Valentine's Day Evening, Women's day, Anniversary day, bonfires, movies, and visits to parks.

A discipleship programme is organized for the youth through workshops and other events which combine fun, food and serious training about being a disciple of Christ which sees evangelism as a priority. Since they are studying or working in a secular place they are taught to share their testimony briefly when an opportunity arises.

Music concerts and competitions in music and dance are organized where the church youth are encouraged to bring their non-Christian friends. The altar call at the end of the programme draws many of them to the cross. Topics like fear and spiritual warfare are also dealt with. The youth are encouraged not to turn anyone away from the faith by poor methods of evangelism where other gods are simply condemned; this is especially important in a pluralistic society like ours.

Youth mission trips are also organized on a regular basis. The team travels to another city or town to share the gospel. Visits to hospitals, old age homes, juvenile homes and orphanages are a regular part of the ministry which gives ample opportunity to reach out to various people with diverse needs. The day is packed with fun events and things that help keep the group serving on their toes. They are put into teams according to their talents and desires, e.g. worship team, dance team, fun and games team, etc. Besides doing their part, each team is equipped to share their testimony and also in praying and counseling youth who respond to the altar call given by the team leader.

Among the many tools mentioned below the prayer walks are also very effective. Teams are sent to different part of the city to pray against spiritual strongholds in those areas and speak salvation silently into the lives of the people of the area. After regular prayer walks are undertaken the team goes back to distribute Christian leaflets and New Testaments to reach the residents.

The tools used in the ministry to be effective in evangelism include:

- Praise and worship concerts
- Theatre (plays and short dramas)
- Camps (Winter, Summer For Jesus)
- Outreach (hospitals, jails, old age homes, and orphanages)
- Workshops and seminars (career and education)

- Corporate fellowships (weekly gatherings, Christmas outreach)
- Campus Ministry
- 1 day *Mataram* (one day retreats)
- Picnics
- Weekly & monthly fasting and praying
- 21 / 30 / 40 days fasting and prayer in January each year
- Youth Sunday
- Prayer Walks
- Fun in the sun (music, sports, creative arts)
- Youth Magazine
- Training for discipleship and effective evangelism

The youth are mentored to realize that life is not just about getting but about giving. Thus to share and to give is taught to become a habit. Truly, evangelism emerges as a lifestyle.

6. Communicating with youth

The goal for the youth ministry God called me to is for every youth to Discover Self, Discover God and Discover the Purpose of Life. The youth ministry annual calendar focuses on these areas and caters to the various areas and needs of the youth.

Where we teach

Besides the regular Saturday youth service where the Word of God is taught on relevant topics, other opportunities are also used to teach. One of the most effective ways of teaching the young people has been through the annual youth camp. During these four days they are apart from the world and open to Heaven. Young people are freed from addictions, bondages, evil spirits and are born again and filled with the Holy Spirit! At the end of the camp a special book to help with devotions is prepared and given to them to help them continue in their meditation on the Word. Parents and Carecell (small group) leaders of the church are also encouraged to come and help in the youth camps. This means we draw on their wisdom and help which leads to more effective ministry.

Young people are also encouraged to join a Yahoo Cell (Youth Alive House of Overcomers) closest to their home as a follow up. These are held midweek in different areas of the city and are very effective, under the guidance of a trained leader. Bible study material is provided to them. They also make good use of Christian videos / movies and this encourages healthy group discussion.

What we teach

The teaching is topical, and the yearly calendar we prepare covers a variety of subjects. It is based on felt needs and the prompting of the Holy Spirit. The teaching emphasis is based on ' i10 '- ten areas of focus to enable growth and discipleship in the ministry. They are: 1) Addicted to the Bible 2) Powerful in Prayer 3) Radical in Worship 4) Baptized in the Holy Spirit 5) Mobilized in Service 6) Sacrificial in Giving 7) Active in Evangelism 8) Baptized in Water 9) Consistent in Testimony 10) Equipped and Empowered.

Relationship

I have realized that successful youth ministry is built on relationship. Time, money and energy invested in young lives are never in vain. Their lives are touched not in a meeting hall but in a coffee house, on long walks and drives, in their homes, over many cups of tea and even on a mission trip. The Chinese proverb rightly says, "If your vision is for a year, plant wheat. If your vision is for ten years, plant trees. If your vision is for a lifetime, plant people".

7. Pastoral care of young people

General pastoral ministry in a church involves assisting in the healthy development of people by creating and maintaining a support system for them at all times. It is different in the youth ministry because we are dealing with young people when they are in a period of transition: they are undergoing changes emotionally, physically, socially, intellectually and spiritually. They are also growing up in a world where there is more danger.

Pastoral care to youth is unique and it is very often difficult to measure effectiveness. Youth pastors need a full range of pastoral ministry skills but don't have the respect or value that the senior pastor has!

Some advice

Marv Penner from Canada, who has more than four decades of experience in youth ministry, answers the question, "What are the three essential things young people are looking for in a Youth Pastor/Leader?":

- Available - They are looking to see how we are available. They need to know where to find us when they need to talk. They need to know we have time, and energy for them.
- Authentic – Are we being real with them? There's nothing they hate more than hypocrisy.
- Accepting – We need to accept them for who they are.

Ezekiel 34:2 provides a strong lesson in pastoral care. "This is what the Sovereign LORD says: Woe to the shepherds of Israel who only take care of themselves! Should not shepherds take care of the flock? You have not strengthened the weak or healed the sick or bound up the injured. You have not brought back the strays or searched for the lost... they were scattered because there was no shepherd".

So the youth pastor needs to have a contagious love for God and the youth. We should have a servant heart and an ability and willingness to listen and learn. A good sense of humor is also essential! We have to build good rapport and find creative ways to encourage them. We need to surprise them with a phone call or a SMS/text.

When you listen to a young person's struggles, give them your full attention. Offer them support where possible. Create trust that will help them open up and tell their story, divulge their emotions, etc. You may not be able to help them on every occasion, so enlist support and, where necessary, refer them to someone else with more expertise.

Some final words of caution

Marv Penner also gives this advice:

- Avoid being alone with young people or creating any situation that could lead to suspicion or misunderstanding.
- Be wise and careful in your use of physical touch. For some it can be badly misinterpreted.
- Remember, your primary relationships should not be intruded.

- Always remember your goal is to make young people stronger by helping them learn to lean on the Lord and not simply on you; we should not become Jesus Christ for them. We should never do for them things that they could do themselves.

8. Working with schools

As we all know, education is a powerful tool to mould young minds and make them what they can be. Though India had a long and glorious past and contributed much in the field of learning, the British played an important role in the introduction of western education through the medium of English during their 200-year rule of our country.

Though the British are criticized for many exploitative acts in India, education was definitely a progressive act of British rule. Three main agencies were responsible for the spread of modern education in India. These were: the foreign Christian missionaries, the British government and progressive Indians. Christian missionaries did extensive work in spreading modern education in India. They started educational institutions, which, along with imparting modern secular education, also introduced Christianity. The legacy continues to this day as many Christian institutions continue to do a noble service in the field of education.

However, the present government in power in India is very keen to return to Hindu culture —a set of myths, beliefs and dogmas— and through which they wish to indoctrinate the country. They have introduced the study of some ancient Hindu Scriptures and the practice of Yoga in schools run by government, and thus has been made compulsory.

Our goal

The goal of our school's campus ministry is this: 'We don't wait for the fish to jump into the boat but we go where the fish are'. In spite of the challenges I've mentioned above, the ministry of Youth Alive (the youth ministry of our church) in campuses has been vibrant for the last 15 years. We have seen hundreds of young people join our Youth group and Church.

I have listed below some of our carefully planned programmes, which are very effective. As a follow up to these sessions we connect young people by email/phone and invite them to our youth service. Some of them are:

- Conducting workshops and seminars in colleges on socially relevant issues like addictions and issues of morality and values
- Having business managers from our church go into college to help equip students for working life and inviting them to apply for jobs
- Seminars on 'How to interview for a job'
- Social Justice Campaigns
- Conducting music/choral classes - irrespective of their creed
- Conducting competitions on national holidays for music/dance, and for bands
- Holding 'food-fests' and carnivals and inviting popular bands to play
- Screening popular movies with Christian values
- Outreach during Christmas – singing of Carols and short dramas on the story of Christmas

We ensure that ministry is backed by a powerful band of praying warriors and we have seen many doors open into many of the institutions. We hold regular Bible fellowship meetings in colleges and have distributed thousands of 'Book of Life' tracts.

My advice and encouragement

A key piece of advice I'd give to youth workers looking for opportunities among students is to be creative, find key contacts in the school through whom you can gain access to students. As most students are searching for meaning/purpose in life, ministry will truly have a great impact on their decisions, their views, their relationship with God and, finally, their eternity.

9. Parents

A teenager once remarked, "Parents are the chains around your ankles until you've managed to either run away, obtain a stable job, die, or turn 18!".

One of the tasks of the youth pastor is dealing with the problems arising from parent-child relationships or, more aptly, 'squabbles'! One way to deal with parents is to get them involved in youth ministry. It gives them a better picture of what their children are doing and stops suspicion and anxiety. But it's not an easy task. As a youth pastor I look at the entire group, but parents can be fixed on their child alone! Since dealing with the parents sometimes seems cumbersome the temptation is often to leave them out! Therefore, in the long run it is better to consider them as a help rather than a hindrance to ministry.

How do we achieve that?

One of the ways to strike a positive note is to acknowledge their importance and speak positively about them and their role when addressing the youth. I also use the family as a context for application when I teach, to impress upon them the value of family. We must consciously make an effort not to create a spirit of 'Us and Them'.

In my interaction with parents I have realized that they also need a lot of affirmation. Though they may complain about their kids, they want to hear good things said about their kids. Some of the words I use when referring to their kids, which they love to hear, is that their child is hard working, insightful, cooperative, helpful, mature, etc.

As parents are the primary spiritual nurturers of their children we often bring them together so they can pray for each other's kids. We even have a programme to equip parents on the common challenges they will face as parents of young people.

It is important to remember that we deal with young people who come from different situations. It could be that some of them are from single parent families or their parents may be unbelievers. Some of their parents attend a different church. Some of them have abusive parents. So we cannot partner with all parents for the spiritual nourishment of their children. We need to evolve different strategies for different parent groups.

In the youth ministry at our church we decided to conduct a one day conference every year for the men and women of our church. We gave them ample opportunity to express themselves through various workshops on a range of topics. This gave us an idea of their strengths and weaknesses. There were many men and women who emerged as leaders from these conferences. This enabled us to use these adults leaders with the young people and bridge the gap between older and younger members of the church family.

The next step was to choose a few couples to help us during the youth camps which are scheduled for 5 days away from the bustle of life. This gives them first-hand experience of understanding the youth – their struggles, their weakness, what makes them happy and in which areas they need encouragement. This has been a great success and has deepened the ministry.

10. Leading a team and developing others

John C. Maxwell rightly said, "Leadership is not about titles, positions, or flowcharts. It is about one life influencing another". God called me to be a leader in the youth ministry while I was still a young executive working with a large company. I have memories and experiences, both good and bad, over my years in youth ministry which have influenced and shaped me to become the leader God called me to be.

My time as a teenager

Being part of YFC (Youth for Christ) clubs, YWAM (Youth with A Mission) and Youth Alive (Youth ministry of my home church) had a great impact on me during my early years. I would have been so lost without being part of youth ministry. I can remember several mentors who impacted my life during those crucial years. I learnt the 'good' and 'bad' of youth ministry by watching these leaders from close quarters. The leaders who impacted my life were not the coolest looking youth leaders but were ordinary people who accepted me as I was and were available to invest in me their time and energy; they showed love and concern and that put me on the path I now walk.

Role models

I learned much from a pastor called Valson Varghese, a man with a passionate heart for reaching out to youth. He impacted many young minds like mine but also pioneered the youth ministry in our church. My youth pastors (Joseph John & John Victor) poured out from their lives into me; they taught and mentored me. The pastor who founded our church, Earl Stubbs, was a true role model. He lived an exemplary life and led like a General on the frontier. His passion for God was contagious. It was he who picked me for the youth leader's post and encouraged me to be in vocational ministry.

Learning from my own experience in youth ministry and from business

When I took over the youth ministry, we averaged an attendance of about 70-100 youth in our weekly group meeting. It grew to a staggering 600 lively bunch of youth known for their talent and passion for God, from all over the twin cities here. I believe I have reaped from the good seed sown by my forerunners. I was fortunate to have a good team of 8-10 people who had a similar love and passion for God. I learnt to lean on God in order to lead the team. We fasted, prayed and planned every week. We made sure God was in every detail of our planning and execution. While we did make a lot of mistakes we had many more successes; because we took a lot of risks, God saw our faith and blessed us, enabling us to grow, both as individuals and as a group.

I learned not only from church and youth ministry circles, but also from industry and corporate business, for example, leadership principles, searching for talent and understanding customer service. I felt like Moses who was educated in the Universities of Egypt. I had this thought running in my mind all through this leadership training period. I knew that one day I was going to use whatever business training I had received, but more directly for the Kingdom of God.

Learning to love and lead like Jesus

Reading the Bible helped me see that the greatest of all leaders and teachers is Jesus. I am learning to live, love and lead like Jesus. This makes my experience as a leader so exciting.

11. You and senior church leaders

On a Saturday evening, back in June 2000, a group of one hundred youngsters had gathered at Youth Alive, our weekly youth service. The atmosphere was as electric as usual but more emotional as it was Johnny's farewell; he had served as the main youth leader faithfully for many years before pursuing his next step. The senior pastor gave a fitting tribute but also chose the same evening to announce Johnny's successor. Me! The announcement had followed an intense one hour discussion the senior pastor and I had together. The occasion took me completely by surprise because I was just one of the volunteer youth leaders; I felt there were better guys for the job.

So my relationship with my senior pastor started off on that very positive note. We gave each other a year to see how things would work out; but that one year multiplied into eight active and fruitful years. We planned & prayed together; partnered on major projects; he would let me preach on Sunday mornings; gave me the freedom I yearned for; he coached me in every sphere of ministry. He pushed me to fulfil God's calling in my life and join the Church full time. If the man could trust me so much, then how could I let him down?

I strongly feel that a major key to successful youth ministry is to build trust with the senior pastor. I often meet youth pastors who have poor regard for their senior pastors. A common complaint is, "He does not understand me". My response is, "God put you under him; that's no mistake". So the onus to build the relationship with your senior pastor is on you! And be sure not to surprise them.

My advice to youth pastors is to pray, plan and partner well. Any imbalance will cause frustration, leading to confusion and even division. Make your senior pastor look good! Your opinion about your senior pastor may actually become the public opinion.

Prayer and planning

Every year, after much prayer, I would plan my annual project calendar and give it to my senior pastor, with all its financial implications. Once signed off, it was an open field. We had worked out a 30:70 ratio of support; 30% by the Church and 70% by the youth.

Partnership

I didn't see the role of youth pastor as a stepping stone to grow! I thought of it more as Aaron & Hur, holding the arms of Moses from dawn till dusk to win the war. I was not to run a parallel ministry or draw up a separate vision, but to rather align myself with the vision of the senior pastor. You may have the most creative of ideas, but if it's not in line with the vision of the senior pastor, then it's a big NO.

If you take time and effort, communicate, trust, and remain accountable, you'll see your relationship flourish with your senior pastor and your youth ministry will grow. Doug Fields, who for many years served as a youth pastor at Saddleback Church in the USA wrote, "You may never be your senior pastor's best friend, but your side of the relationship ought to be encouraging & healthy. Are you doing your part?".

Chapter 6

Matt Gregor from Wales

My chapter is dedicated to the incredible volunteer youth ministry team I have served and serve with - thank you so much.

1. My background and how I got into youth ministry

I grew up in a small town in the middle of Wales, a small Celtic nation of around 3 million people and 12 million sheep! Known as the 'land of song' we host a large national festival of music and poetry every year. A large minority speak not only English but Welsh. We can claim one of the oldest unbroken literary traditions in Europe and a world class rugby team. The well-known pirate of the Caribbean, Henry Morgan, was born in Wales. Famous Welsh actors and singers today include Tom Jones, Anthony Hopkins and Catherine Zeta-Jones.

I had great Christian parents who took me and my three sisters and brother along to an Assemblies of God Pentecostal Church in mid-Wales. I remember committing my life to God as a child at a meeting led by an Argentinian evangelist called Luis Palau. We then moved as a family to Cardiff, south Wales when I was in my early teens. I didn't have a huge connection with any youth group growing up but had lots of adult Christian friends who, looking back, were a great influence on my life. When a student, age 19, I started attending the City Temple Elim Pentecostal Church, a city centre church of about 700 people. I quickly started helping with the youth ministry. On graduation I was asked to come onto the staff at our Church as youth pastor, and although reluctant at first I saw God use me throughout the years.

Very quickly the number of young people between 11 and 16 grew to about twenty, and with the help of some friends things were going great. We did a few ministry weekends away and attended larger summer camps which consolidated the group and solidified some key values we were to establish.

We quickly realised that underneath all the fun we were having we wanted a solid foundation of love for God and consequently love for worship, love for Scriptures, and love for people. On these broad values we have tried to build the youth ministry. I was hugely blessed with an incredibly supportive and gracious church leadership who wanted to see me grow and helped to fan into flame the gifts God had put in me. I think the leadership and parents in churches form a very powerful component for youth leaders to partner with for successful youth ministry.

In the early years I was much more focused on people than programs and struggled with some of the administration that goes along with youth ministry. I would still much rather help young people face to face in a very immediate and tangible way than plan in advance and think through all the possibilities with rotas and getting equipment organised. Having said that, after twelve years in youth ministry and some natural maturity I am much more on top of organisation!

In 2010 I was ordained as a minister in the Elim Pentecostal Church. I felt this was important since it added more weight to youth ministry in the Church and also because, in my experience, a lot of the ministry stuff in Church had been about encouraging and helping adults, namely our volunteer teams, parents, teachers and other genuine, good people – normal church members! It is difficult to be on a pastoral team at Church for a few years and not love the people!

I am now in my mid-thirties and married to Hannah. We have a young daughter called Chloe and a son called Joseph. I love our Church and seeing people come to faith, releasing people in their gifting and also helping other youth leaders along in their journey. It has been important in youth ministry to talk to boys about English Premiership football (!), but my real love has always been motorcars. I enjoy all things cars, working on them, driving them, talking about them and even trading them.

Whilst I was in my teens, as a family growing up we didn't have lots of money. So I have a heart for young people with difficult family situations, especially those without positive male role models in their lives. I always try to look out for and sensitively help young people from challenging financial backgrounds. It's amazing how God uses things in our lives which we didn't particularly enjoy going through in order to help others!

2. Looking after your own soul

On starting out in youth ministry I naively thought that I would have more hours than I could imagine communing with God and soaking in His presence. I'm now used to the question people ask, "What do you do in the week?". I guessed I would be praying for the flock and deep in Bible study. It was a shock to me that life was just the same with deadlines, demands and interruptions throughout the week - just the same as in other employment. Some of the rhythms of youth ministry in terms of weekends, evenings and early mornings did present a challenge to my own daily time with God. At the start of the day I try to have time with God before my mind starts racing with what needs to be attended to.

Bible reading

I personally connect with God mostly through Bible reading and tend to read it until something jumps off the page at me; then I like to meditate on that theme, or a story or word that is highlighted. A few years ago I started to get a new Bible each year so I could mark each page that I read; I found this tremendously helpful when wondering what to read! That simple technique has helped me discover new insights from Scripture rather than leaning on the same thoughts I scribbled into the Bible however many years ago. Sometimes I think I've read something recently in the Bible, only to realise that I couldn't have given the date on the front of my new Bible. The daily discipline of opening the Bible brings a healthy walk with God. I don't feel like opening the Bible every day, but God speaks more to someone who opens the Bible every day than someone who only reads it when they feel like it.

I have found some of the most significant youth ministry moments come out of my own time with God in prayer and Bible reading. I tend to read and pray with pen in hand; the number of times the Holy Spirit has dropped someone's name or a great idea into my mind have been incredible. When we get some time with God to pray for youth and our own situations he often gives us keys that open doors we would struggle to unlock on our own. I also find running and walking have helped me to pray and process thoughts and ideas. In his book *Axiom: Powerful Leadership Proverbs*, Bill Hybels talks about the value of a good idea.

Forgiveness

Another major way of looking after your own soul is practising forgiveness. In youth ministry you will get plenty of opportunities to practice forgiveness and I have adopted the mantra "Today I forgive everyone of everything they have ever done to me". Our soul is kept healthy by letting go of resentment and practising forgiveness. Our relationships with others are so key in our relationship with God, but so often overlooked. When someone wrongs us or misunderstands us, or (if you are anything like me) when we misjudge someone or something, coming back to forgiveness is the key to staying healthy with the Lord. The apostle John asks how we can love God whom we can't see if we can't love our brother who we can see (1 John 4:20). Freeing myself from resentment and grudges is one of the biggest ways of maintaining a healthy soul.

3. Singleness, marriage and children

I have been single for most of my time in youth ministry and loved the freedom to throw myself into youth and Church ministry. I could stay up late at night after youth programmes or Church services chatting with young people and the youth team without having to worry about getting home for anyone.

If you want to get married

Over the years, I dated a few different girls and tried to treat each one with care and integrity. Dating different girls helped me realise some of the personality traits I wanted in a wife. I remember thinking I wanted someone who was attractive, fun and on fire for God! A huge part of our ministry was fun and I wanted a wife who would smile and enjoy the journey, which is exactly what I got. The Bible says in Psalm 100:2, "Worship the Lord with gladness, come before him with joyful songs".

Hannah and I met and married in nine months. For me, she was very different to anyone else I had met, and in a great way I knew she was the one for me. She is gorgeous, great company, great fun and on fire for God. She has clear leadership ability and always honours me, and the Church. There have been times in ministry where I have wanted to shelter her from some of the things going on in Church life, or from the incessant demands that vocational ministry can make. She has volunteered with me in youth ministry, but I didn't let her serve over and above what I would expect other volunteers to do. I very much believe in the 'long game' of youth ministry and never wanted volunteers to commit so much that they were good for nothing in other areas of their lives.

With a wife, young daughter and son I am now in a completely different season of life; but I approach my new responsibilities and privileges as I have every other season in life and enjoy them.

4. Organising yourself and your ministry

I was the classic disorganised youth pastor at the start; it did not come naturally to me. But I realised that, as the youth team leader, the youth pastor doesn't have to be the best in the room at everything - that includes organisation. A secure leader gets a good team on their side. I also realised quickly that it is less work overall if you have a plan in advance, and the outcome is that what you achieve is of a higher quality.

What do you want to achieve?

Organising a youth ministry programme comes from first working out what you are trying to achieve. The programme is a vehicle to get you somewhere. Use it to grow disciples, reach the lost, equip the saints, etc. Some people who are disorganised blame the Holy Spirit for their laziness. For example they say, "What if the Holy Spirit moves on the evening we are meeting?". But it is an excuse. Can't the Holy Spirit also speak to the leader or speaker months or weeks in advance as well as on the night in question? When we plan in advance we can engage more people in what we are doing. We can also communicate better what we are trying to achieve.

Prioritise

Put time for your devotional life first. Many interruptions come into life whether you are salaried by a Church or not. Your devotional lifestyle is yours to nurture and fan into flame. In fact you should pour fuel (!) on the fire with worship, prayer and God's word filling your heart. Put God first with quality uninterrupted time with him. The Holy Spirit will drop thoughts and ideas and situations and people into your mind to pray for and to connect with.

I write a 'to do' list where I try to prioritise what I am doing and put the most important thing first rather than the easiest task first. Mark Twain wrote, "Eat a live frog first thing in the morning and nothing worse will happen to you the rest of the day". In other words, do the biggest, worst or most dreaded task first and you will have the satisfaction of knowing you've tackled the most challenging task of your day. Don't procrastinate.

Retreats and camps

When organising retreats or camps, some of the things I do include: a drawer for all money coming in and out (I'd even write on bank notes to help me remember where they came from); Excel spreadsheets with lots of information on them (using the same spreadsheet as last year helps you remember what to bring); put everyone's number (parents, etc) in your phone as it is far more accessible if you need it during a youth activity or in an emergency; a spreadsheet with each expense claim so you can remember what you have and haven't been reimbursed for.

Communication

Get information out to people about what is going on. Important information needs repeated in different ways. For example, for retreats and weekends away do not just distribute leaflets and letters but make and/or show a promotional video, get youth to talk about how good it was last year and how good it will be this year, get banners up in the youth room or Church, get posters up where youth or parents will see the information, print T-shirts advertising the event, advertise discounts for those who book early, do a competition to see who can bring the most people along, use social media. Don't do one of these things - do them all!

Parents and other adults

Letters to parents about trips need to contain the time and place, where and when you leave from, and where and when you arrive back, how much money - and anything else - they need. Share this information with parents and team and youth. If you are being asked the same question by 2 or 3 different people then you probably didn't communicate clearly enough! Ask parents to help. Often the parents care about youth ministry and will help with communication, driving, extra funds, extra volunteers, cooking and hospitality. Use the parents because they want you to succeed! If something goes wrong and is awkward or embarrassing then tell your boss/line manager as soon as possible so they can help minimise damage; you can plan on how to fix it together.

5. Keeping your evangelism edge sharp

It is sometimes a challenge to keep your mission edge sharp when people of influence in the Church tend to listen primarily to the parents' needs and demands; parents can often prioritise their own children's happiness rather than reaching those outside of the kingdom of God. So here are some of the things I want to share with you that have helped keep our evangelism edge sharp. The youth ministry should be an evangelism engine of the local church!

Encourage people to bring friends

I have observed that 20% of the congregation bring 80% of new people along to church. So I would encourage you to celebrate and give profile to those people who are bringing their friends along. The things you celebrate and give attention to will grow, so encourage those who are doing what we all ought to be doing! Young people that aren't saved won't come knocking at your door, so we need to keep them in the front of our mind when planning our programmes and events. No lost person complains that they haven't been witnessed to for many months. Do some research – ask young people both in and outside of your church why people don't come along. Make the survey a genuine information gathering exercise and seek to listen and respond to what you find out.

Get away

Young people tend to make commitments of faith at retreats and camps and special events. The relationships and a sense of belonging are important, as is getting away from home; all these thing are good for giving youth a chance to think about the gospel. Most non Church young people come to Church and to faith through their friends inviting them.

Other tools

In our Church we use baptism services. People in the Church invite friends along, and they come! The combination of a great welcome, a clear gospel presentation and testimony makes for a good opportunity for new people to come. I have friends who live-stream all their Church services and invite people locally to join them online for a few weeks before the baptism service. If you have the opportunity, then school assemblies are also great for throwing the gospel net wide. Use John 3:16 as a verse to train young people to explain the gospel to their friends.

Our personal responsibility

I have sometimes been guilty of only leading people to the Lord at the front of a meeting but expecting the others to go and do all the personal evangelism. But as a witness of God's goodness I try to share my faith in every area of life, not just when I'm doing youth work or leading a meeting. Recently I was talking to a man who said he didn't go to church any more. As we were talking about parenting I had the opportunity to ask him if he still prayed. He said he did, and was a little surprised that I had asked. Did I ask the right question? I am not sure if I did, but what I do know is that I had a great opportunity to talk about the goodness of God with him, and I did! If we can be people who are continually talking about the goodness of God everywhere we go then young people will pick up on that and think that is normal! We can always have excuses not to talk about the goodness of God, for example, "I'm busy with church work" or "I go to the Bible study" or "I give financially". The command of the Lord Jesus is simple and clear: "Go and make disciples of all nations".

6. Communicating with youth

If you eat your favourite meal from your favourite restaurant every day then it won't be long before that is your least favourite meal, however good it is. I think the teaching plan for youth ministry is a bit like a menu where the variety of approach, style, presentation and person all help keep young people engaged. Let me encourage you to have a variety of approaches to communicating the gospel in order to keep young people engaged and to appeal to different people in your group.

Some ways of doing this are to have guest speakers, stand-alone topics, topical series, current issues, Bible teaching from a book of the Bible, testimonies, thematic teaching from a current issue or about something everyone is talking about, and of course an 'any questions' evening. A good rule of thumb for teaching, I find, is to have a 'Bible in one hand and a newspaper in the other' - the then and now of connecting today with the Bible, in the context of young people today. It is listening to young people and their issues, and listening to what God wants to say; this is key to developing a helpful and engaging teaching plan. I have used Christian devotional books as a springboard to inspire a series, or Christian movies to help explain a passage. I use the Bible DVD a lot to help young people imagine what is happening in a specific passage.

Develop a plan

If you get a solid skeleton structure in place for maybe six months in advance then you will be able to deliver a higher quality of teaching than if you just live from week to week. Plan in advance and you can schedule guest speakers, equip young people to speak, find resources and illustrations for your topic, produce publicity about your theme and get your team on board with where you are going. Not having a long term plan will actually give you more work and stress, and with a lower quality result. However charismatic and interesting you are, if you are speaking to the same young people each week without preparation then it won't be long until they are bored of the same shallow stories and themes that come into your head on the spur of the moment. Some people use the "Holy Spirit moving" excuse for not wanting to prepare. If the Holy Spirit wants to lead us then he is welcome to, and we believe, as leaders, that he is leading us. He does sometimes speak to us on the evening of a youth meeting, but - unbelievably for some youth leaders - he can also speak days and weeks before the programme when you sit down to prepare and plan!

Images, stories and change

When speaking to young people, I personally like lots of pictures on my PowerPoint (or other software) slides rather than lots of words. It is often a battle to keep young people engaged and pictures can help spark the imagination. Your major life events, both good and bad, will always be powerful tools to help shape young people's thinking and lives. We are real people communicating to real people with their hopes and dreams, aspirations, disappointments, sorrow and joy. We are living letters (2 Corinthians 3:2) that young people are reading. When we say to God "use me" we are offering him our whole lives. Our weakness and struggles (at appropriate times) can often bring the most help and comfort to others. Keep the end goal in mind, which is to see lives transformed rather than simply educating young people. Andy Stanley talks about this further in his excellent book *Communicating for a Change*.

7. Pastoral care of young people

One of the best ways to do pastoral care is in small groups. I haven't always found small groups work in different homes because young people also like the larger group feel of seeing each other too, so we have dedicated a significant slot in our weekly programme for small group time together. For you, this may be as simple as splitting the boys and the girls up. In this way you can grow larger in overall numbers and not lose out on the depth of relationships of small groups. I always tend to split small groups up by gender and school year with a little bit of flexibility for the local situation. In this way the youth are with the same people each week and, if they are in the youth ministry for years, are with the same people for the long term.

It is also great to have the same small group leaders in the same group each week. For example, Lydia has the year 9 girls (age 13/14) and Jason has year 8 boys (age 12/13) every week. A small group leader can be more aware of issues that arise and has a depth of relationship through chatting and praying each week together with young people; they will have a stronger relationship with their group than the overall leader does. Set up small groups and release leaders to do pastoral care. Try to do it all out of relationship rather than out of a structure. If you need to challenge a young person about something it is much easier if you have first developed relationship with them. Small groups help a lot with this.

Goals, behaviour and care

Remember the goals and vision of the youth ministry. My definition of discipleship is very simple: becoming like Jesus. The simpler that things are defined, the easier they are to achieve! Reward those who are making tangible progress towards those goals. If bad behaviour and dysfunction means young people get attention then young people will tend to behave in such a way to get that attention. Most ministries tend to allocate leaders' time to those behaving badly instead of those behaving in a godly way. This is surely an incentive for bad behaviour and will be counter-productive.

Try to define those who fall into your sphere of pastoral care and those who do not. Some kids come to all your programmes, are at the core of what you are doing, and so there is plenty of space available for them to be cared for. Some kids do not come to anything for six months - do you have pastoral oversight for them too?

Adults and the wider church

If you have a strong and godly youth team then the young people will have lots of godly role models whom they see in and around church life. This is important because the main youth leader cannot connect with every single young person. Some volunteers are there each week, others may help a few times a year. The young people will become more round-ed as disciples, and in their experience of receiving pastoral care, when they receive from all these different types of people. The whole church is responsible for the young people, not just the youth team.

8. Working with schools

Whilst working at a church there is sometimes the expectation that you are at that church, sitting at your desk. This is not youth work or ministry. If a youth pastor is full time and not going into schools then I often wonder what exactly they are doing with their time. Maybe they are engaged in other church activities that are good, but these may be drawing them away from youth ministry. Young people spend all day in school so, if you can, go and meet them in school during the day. If not, then meet them after school. Young people are helped by relationship and time with you significantly more than by an email or a text from you.

Trust and relationship

If legally you can gain access to schools, first build up trust and rela-tionship with teachers, etc. Find out what teachers or schools need and help them with those needs. When you are useful and helpful to a school the teachers and young people will want to listen to what you have got to say. It may not sound too 'spiritual' helping young people learn to read, helping with mentoring, or offering to go on school trips as an additional adult but we are to be salt and light in the world and help where we can. It is worth it.

When we are helpful and useful to a school then we will have opportunities to talk about the goodness of God and show his love and compassion. Young people love to see their youth pastor in their school, and as you walk the corridors and meet young people there will be lots of opportunities to encourage youth you haven't seen for a while and meet some that are about to connect with your church.

Some of the things I have done

In Cardiff each week I was in a 'Church in Wales' (church run but state-funded) school, and as part of a weekly opportunity I led 'parish prayers' where clergy from all over the city would have 10 minutes with the youth from their parish. What a great opportunity to bring good news and encouragement!

One Easter we bought Easter eggs for every teacher in a couple of schools where lots of our young people attended to thank them for all they did; the response was incredible! Young people love to see the friendship and conversations between youth ministers from different churches. It is fantastic to model to young people that although we are from different churches we are on the same side; when we win they win! One school I knew had a 'leader board' on how they thought different pastors were doing! It is so powerful when we collaborate and show a school unity between church leaders and youth ministers across the city.

We often helped host a group from Youth for Christ (a para-church ministry) or facilitated a special Easter or Christmas presentation. Some religious education departments in schools in the UK like pupils to tour different places of worship, so open the doors of your building and get the drinks and snacks in, let the kids take their 'selfies' on their phones standing in your baptism pool and in the pulpit. It's God's house anyway and he wants all people to come home.

9. Leading a team and developing others

Don't assume people will say "No". Ask them because they may well say "Yes". The whole church is there to bring glory to God, so everyone should be serving one another and helping reach out to the lost. Assist people in finding opportunities to do that by asking them to help. Get adults connecting into the youth ministry at different levels. Some people can commit every few weeks, so don't just pick those who can help every week. For some adults, 4 hours a week will be too much but they may be able to help out every 2 or 3 weeks. Some team members can connect each term, or once a year to help with an outreach or social event or a residential camp. As someone who now has a young family I am even more aware of the demands upon parents. I am even more grateful of the sacrifice and commitment so many people made into youth ministry, which I was definitely not aware of before I was a parent! Getting people better than you on your team is the best thing to do – it doesn't make you look bad, it makes you look great!

Building a team

Seek genuine relationship with people on the team and potential team people. Try to make the team relationships part of your life so the team are genuinely close friends of yours. If you pastor and lead the team well then the team will pastor the young people. If the main youth leader is trying to do all the youth work then there is only a limited amount that they can do, but if they are enabling and equipping a great team then the influence will be so much greater. One of the things we did for team training was read a specialist book together and discuss the chapter each couple of weeks (like you could do with this book!). Another was to reflect on how the youth ministry was that evening - what went well, what should we change for the future. It is powerful to reflect on how the program went because often the team have fabulous ideas which, when implemented, raise their level of involvement and ownership in the ministry.

Misunderstanding

At times I have placed so much emphasis on teamwork that a mentor suggested that perhaps I needed to do more myself. It may have looked like I was not doing a lot. I was thrilled and annoyed at the same time. But it was really a compliment because he was saying I was the best communicator to the young people. I did what I did best and helped others on the team play their part. What a joy for volunteers to serve in the local church in such significant ways, rather than a full time youth pastor getting to do all the best bits. A famous leadership proverb says, "The only thing worse than training your people and losing them is not training them and keeping them!".

10. Parents

I am constantly amazed at how many youth leaders struggle with their relationships with their own parents and then expect young people to honour and love their parents. Apart from dysfunctional situations we have a clear principle from Scripture, "Children, obey your parents". We should do all we can to set an example of how that is a good and wholesome thing to do. For us as adults it is all down to respect. So try your best to speak to all parents with love, respect and honour in order to model to young people that is how they are to speak to their parents. It seems Hollywood sometimes portrays parents as total idiots only good for funding their kids' quest for happiness. This is worlds apart from how God wants young people to treat their parents.

You're all on the same side

Young people will spend immensely more time with their parents than with any youth leader. Ask what would help the parents. How can you best serve them? Parents and families tend to have busy diaries and need a long lead in to different events coming up. Give them as much notice as possible about events, residential events, etc, that are coming up. Tell them what the event is, where it is, how much it costs, what young people need to bring, when it is, what time it starts what time it finishes and how they could help. If something goes wrong and their child is hurt or upset then, as we say in our country, 'grasp the nettle' (a stinging plant) and get on with making the call to apologise and explain what happened. It will sting but it is better than allowing the issue to linger.

Work together for the greater good, putting frustrations aside and focus on your shared goals. Parents are supportive of you more than you realise and want you to win - their kids are the most precious thing in their lives. With young people from Christian homes, particularly, you have parents who want them to grow up loving God and connected in church. A young person's faith is not solely a parent or youth leader's responsibility; we as a body all take the responsibility and serve together.

11. You and senior church leaders

It's the conversations and decisions at a senior level that have a profound effect on youth ministry, so it's worth spending time and energy getting those relationships right. We lead up, as well as down and across, in terms of the organisational responsibility chart.

As well as leading a youth ministry team and young people we also have incredible influence on those senior leaders who lead us. So there is a challenge for us to be a total blessing to them. You may have a lot of work to do in youth ministry, but it is a priority both for the safety of your job and for the harmony of the team that you think through how you can be a positive influence to those who lead you!

Youth pastor x 10

I often ask myself if 10 of me would be a total blessing or someone's worst nightmare come true! So make yourself in attitude, actions, love and purity a dream-come-true-youth-minister for whoever it is you are serving, because you know it is ultimately for the Lord Jesus Christ.

Specific advice

If you've made a mistake then own up - don't hide it. Treat everyone with respect and love. Try to be yourself. Show them the respect of listening. Imagine yourself in their shoes. Find out what their definition of success for your responsibilities in youth ministry would look like, and talk that through with them so you are going after the same thing.

Chapter 7
Zeeshan James from Pakistan

My chapter is dedicated to my Mom.

1. My background and how I got into youth ministry

I live in Karachi, a major international city in Pakistan with a population of over 20 million people. It is known as the gateway to our country as it has major sea and dry ports for trade and tourism. The total population of the country is around 183 million, of which 97% would say they are Muslim (all sects). The majority of the other 3% are Christian or Hindu, with the remainder being Buddhist, Sikh, Zoroastrian, Jewish or Atheist. Christianity existed in the area long before the birth of the nation of Pakistan; the apostle Thomas was the only one to reach the Indian sub-continent with the gospel and that gospel is still spreading by the grace of Almighty God.

Pakistan is quite different from what you may think. We are considered by other nations as being aggressive, full of terrorists and fanatics, etc. But it is due to a religious fundamentalist mindset held by only a few, although it is increasing day by day. Pakistan may be very diverse, multi-cultural and multi-ethnic, but love for children, honor for women, care for the oppressed, and respect for elders are regarded as primary values. Our national language is Urdu and the official language is English. The presence of God is everywhere, and I have felt it since I was ten years old!

My background

I am a Pakistani by nationality and Christian by faith. I mention this because most people living in the sub-continent here who become Christians come from a different background. About ten generations ago, my ancestors were introduced to Christ. So I was born and raised in Christian faith and with Pakistani values. Growing up, my Mom was very loving and had a strong God-fearing faith. She raised me and my two elder brothers as best as she could, teaching us good manners, helping us differentiate between good and bad, and encouraging us in daily devotions in the morning and before going to bed, and often in the middle of the night. She taught us the Word of God as a preacher, and corrected as a teacher.

I have been married for seven years to Suniya. She is a blessing and a great support in my youth ministry as she encourages the young women. She completed a Master's degree in English Literature and teaches at a college in Karachi. We serve together in youth ministry, study at our theology classes together, pray together, see fruit and are blessed together each day. We have two beautiful kids, Serena Zoe James (7 years) and Ezekiel Zuriel James (4 years).

An early calling

I sensed from an early age that I was called to work with young people. Even during my early days in church I was very much involved in volunteering with youth groups. I soon found myself planning and preparing new, innovative activities for young people. I also made plans to reach young people not connected with the church. I worked closely with clergy staff, elders and senior youth leaders to reach these young people. I faced both discouragement and often encouragement; in both scenarios I required self-motivation.

I worked as the President of Youth Ministry at Christ Church, Drigh Road Parish, Karachi where God used my talents and prepared me for bigger challenges. This gave me opportunities to change the mindset of many who were resisting youth ministry. During that time I became a Youth Advisory Panel Member for the United Nations Populations Fund (UNFPA).

My work on the Youth Advisory Panel broadened my horizons. I encouraged the young people by saying this and equipping them to think along the same lines. It brought a big change in our church youth as the youth ministry became their platform to express, share, learn, explore, revive and encourage each other through the word of God.

I always believe 'God has a bigger plan' whenever anything goes against my human will, so after I left my role with UNFPA I moved to Islamabad, the capital city, for my Master's degree studies. My passion for youth work was growing and I noticed that young people there did not have leadership. They lacked vision and focus, and so with support of elder brothers and like-minded peers we managed to start 'Rising Youth Ministry' with the vision of 'Paying back to the community'. It is part of the Not-for-Profit Organization 'IMPACT - Pakistan' (International Mission for Poverty Alleviation and Community Transformation) with a vision for empowering the less-privileged.

'Rising Youth Ministry' formed a team, set down some values, brainstormed, and prayerfully we planned, focusing on the needs of young people across the entire city. After completing my Master's degree I returned to my home city Karachi and started working with the Diocesan Youth Council of the Diocese of Karachi, Church of Pakistan and started 'Rising Youth Ministry' there, and in other cities as well, each with their own locally raised budgets.

It is now 16 years that God has been using me among the young people. The journey started from my local church youth group, then from one city to another. My work has also taken me abroad to countries such as India, Nepal, China, England, Turkey, Cyprus, Germany, Scotland, Malaysia, United Arab Emirates and the United States to meet young leaders. All this is done by God's grace alone, who refines me, strengthens me and helps me overcome my weaknesses!

2. Looking after your own soul

Often, many of us are on the wrong track. Although we work hard to make a success of our ministry, see large numbers of youth, we can still we feel that something is missing. We need it to bring to the Lord in prayer. It is quite common for this to happen to those serving in youth ministry. Once we bring it to God we can experience a revitalisation of our faith; blessings flow out through us and revive others too.

Youth ministry is not common in Pakistan. The spiritual needs of young people are not seen as important in society or the local church. Often they are ignored or paid little attention. Youth leaders, therefore, face major challenges such as discouragement, de-motivation, threats and fear.

Problems and how to overcome them

Discouragement can come in the form of discouraging remarks, criticism, and unproductive attitudes; the effect of these can tear apart the enthusiasm of young leaders and demoralize them. De-motivation develops if there is continuous rejection. Resistance to youth ministry and hurdles eventually damage self esteem and ministry momentum. Fear can creep in in a subtle way because it comes from within. Fear can also develop from being rejected by family, leadership problems or pressure from peers. One of the biggest challenges we face in Pakistan is the fundamentalist elements who are at large and keep track of the activities of other faiths.

Being threatened in youth ministry may sound unusual to many cultures, but doing ministry in Pakistan, in a multicultural and multi-faith society, is a very real responsibility that one has to deal with. The nature of such threats can be difficult to assess but we should not ignore them. Churches and parachurch organizations are often threatened by religious extremists. Back in 2012, I was being followed everywhere I went - from home to work, from work to church, and other places; everywhere I went, in fact. One night, I got back home and was tired; I did not leave my car safely in the garage but parked it outside. In the morning I found a window smashed and had to check my files, documents, laptop bag and every corner of the car to verify that nothing had been stolen. It hadn't.

Around six months later someone shot at my car, hitting a door. I have no idea where the shot came from, but thank God I was unharmed. I changed the route I drove and also changed my car. I told my family what happened, and they encouraged me. I also read the same day the Bible passage Romans 8:31-39 where it says, "nothing can separate us from the love of God".

God and our responsibility

To overcome fear you need to bring it in prayer to God. He always answers prayer and empowers us to accept these challenges and helps us to transform discouragement into encouragement, de-motivation into motivation, and fear and threats into opportunities! Almost anyone can encourage their own soul as an inner life discipline. You need to address discouragement with the positivity of God's word. A discouraging situation can be turned upside down. Young people in Pakistan often take no initiative and have no self motivation. It is important for them to know how to encourage their own soul and become motivated. They need to learn how to 'break the ice' and not have someone do it for them. Therefore, knowing how to encourage my own soul and teach young people to do it too is important.

3. Singleness, Marriage and Children

In Pakistan, cultural traditions vary greatly across the country. Illustrating each of them would be complex and take away from the main point of this section.

In general, there are no cultural traditions that encompass being single. Yet some people can be single for many years. In my country the eldest child in the family often has to remain single until they have fulfilled their responsibility to the rest of the family; they are expected to look after younger siblings and support them in their education until they are married. This might include helping pay for any wedding expenses including the celebrations, guests, entertainment and, in the case of a female sibling, the dowry.

Arranged marriages, but with consent

Marriages can be arranged by parents *and* involve the partners. My marriage was arranged, but with my consent. After my elder brothers left home and settled with their families my father asked me if there was anyone whom I would like to marry. I was not in any sort of relationship and so I allowed my father to pick someone for me. He consulted with me before finalizing everything. I needed someone with the same level of education as me, with a clear passion for youth ministry, and willing to support me in my call. I felt blessed to go with my father's choice as he picked a girl who was the daughter of a Bishop. She had compassion and wanted to serve others; she was already involved in youth work in the diocese. Suniya and I had already interacted on the National Youth Forum twice before we got engaged. We were married 18 months later, in January 2009.

In Pakistan, and in most Asian countries we have a saying, "One and one makes eleven, not two". After our marriage, Suniya added value and blessings to 'Rising Youth Forum' and 'IMPACT – Pakistan' as it became not only my call but hers as well. We started focusing on women and started to see more women coming to our events.

Children

After having children, the pace slows down. But after the children learn to walk you realise you have a new member of the team to encourage and help you in organizing things! Our first child is often around us while we are hosting; they help energize us and often participate with team members during games and extra-curricular activities. Likewise, our second child enjoys being with us during youth work, sharing at annual dinners and visiting new places. We have noticed that they enjoy being with new friends and find it easy to communicate and mingle with others. I am not sure how much they will be involved in youth work when they are older, but one thing is for sure: they have tasted God's Word in their earliest days and are gifted with many talents which will develop in the years to come.

4. Organising yourself and your ministry

Organising yourself is a challenging task, especially if you have to perform several roles in life, such as living at home, being a sibling, parent, spouse, neighbor, boss, subordinate, co-worker, peer, group leader, team player, or volunteer, etc. This will depend on how much responsibility you have in addition to home and work.

When you start out you may look at others who are procrastinating or failing to keep their commitments. It may be very easy to criticize and think you will not repeat the same mistakes, but once in the role you may see yourself doing the same! It is a common mistake we all make and I did it too; but with a little more focus you can overcome this and become more organised.

As we talked about in the previous section it is easy to become discouraged, and many youth leaders need to learn to become more organised as well as becoming better at motivating themselves. Often youth leaders are considered to be "Baby Pastors'. It is a very casual taunt even if we are well organised and present ourselves well to others. It may be due to the other person being biased, or it may be that we deserve it because we are not proactive in our approach!

No one can 'manage' time, and as the old saying goes, "Time and tide wait for no man". True, but we can definitely manage ourselves and use our time positively.

My advice

Here are some tips I give to students, team members and volunteers.

They really help in organising yourself and your ministry and so avoid getting into a panic.

Always put first things first. In other words always put God first. Prior to planning, prayerfully seek God's help in executing things efficiently. I find that my daily devotions and meditation are the best way to begin a day. Consequently, my daily routine becomes more synchronised and I become more productive and effective.

Use a good diary. If your church setting is more traditional use a lectionary that marks special church seasons and Sunday services. This will help you prioritise your tasks and meet the deadlines ahead of time.

Focus on needs. You should be well aware of your personal needs, your team's needs and the needs of your youth ministry as a whole.

Determine your priorities. If you consciously decide what those are, it will help to balance youth work vs non-youth work activities. You can then learn to say "No" to non-essential things, and "Yes" to important things.

Be willing to learn at any stage, and from any one. Humility helps us in numerous ways and creates space for more good fruit in us; it benefits us for a life-time.

Do it! We can read several management books or self-management techniques that add value to our knowledge, but actually *doing* it is key; it is as we actually start getting organised that we begin to change.

5. Keeping your evangelism edge sharp

Pakistan is known as one of the most dangerous countries in the world. Christians are under threat and often have to face difficulties in the form of persecution and allegations of blasphemy. Due to these factors the Church at times feels that evangelism is a sensitive and complex subject. Various strategies are adopted and several ministries, especially those for or led by young people, have made major advances. Even so, getting young people together is easier than achieving the goal of evangelism.

Some resources

Christian young people in Pakistan face many faith-related queries and debates at work from their co-workers and peers. People need answers to real-life questions. Whatever evangelism methods we use, the area of apologetics is key. Printed literature with facts and figures is also a handy tool to have. Believers use these during evangelism training at conferences because they can then recall this information during discussions with non-believers. Many today prefer to use social media, which has its own merits. Inspirational evangelists are a great resource for 'question and answer' sessions that help clarify the ambiguities faced by young people. But perhaps the most important tool in evangelism is your own life.

The character of Christ in the believer is the greatest resource

Mahatma Gandhi was a very simple, but great, revolutionary hero. Here are two painful quotes from him which we should reflect on, and overcome where we are lacking:

"I like your Christ, I do not like your Christians. Your Christians are so unlike your Christ";
"If Christians would really live according to the teachings of Christ, as found in the Bible, all of India would be Christian today".

Believers can face tough and stressful times. By being encouraged and made strong in Christ believers can show Christ-like character: patience, humbleness, courage, obedience, commitment, and not complain as much. This would help answer Gandhi's challenge! Once they are strongly rooted in Christ, we find that young people become better at being more self-motivated to spread the gospel and share the Great Commission through their values and behavior; they reflect Christ through their lives as a living gospel. Although our society is very diverse and multicultural the believer is still a 'non-resident' in this world; they should not adopt the values of the society they live in but gradually transform it through the way they live and work. This is a great testimony to those who do not yet believe.

For example, through the collective efforts of 'IMPACT – Pakistan' and 'Rising Youth Forum' we have seen many lost sheep brought back; it wasn't us, but part of God's divine plan. God knows how, where, when and whom to use. Many drug addicts, youth who have left church, hooligans, political workers, etc, have repented and joined us, working zealously. Once such worker was miraculously saved during a bomb blast at a political procession of his favorite political leader (who was assassinated later that year). When he opened his eyes in his hospital bed he did not know what had happened. I was the first person to call him. I assured him that it was God who saved him and wanted to use him to work among Christian youth and tell his story. We now use his interpersonal, technical, and analytical skills in logistics and to organize our events and a lot more.

In summary

During my school days I used to share small pocket-sized gospels with my non-believer friends whenever they had a question or concern about Christianity. By the time I was at University the 'Jesus Film' DVD was a more effective tool because it made it easy for others to get to know the real story of Jesus. Now with the passage of time in youth ministry I have realised that real evangelism cannot be carried out just using helpful tools, be they literature or media. It is through one's own Christian values and attributes that we reflect Christ in our daily routine at school, at work, while travelling, in happy times, during difficulties, in trouble, in prosperity, in fact in every way, even in persecution.

6. Communicating with youth

The modern teen in Pakistan is very different from those in the past. Methods that worked long ago do not work so well today. Young people now want more than just words. In Pakistan, young people look for facts and figures, they want to know how they can touch and feel what they are being taught, and how they can practise it. They assess, evaluate and measure what they are being taught. These changes are positive. It makes it easier for youth leaders to assess what ingredients to put into their teaching and how to best communicate God's Word.

When I was a teen I always had certain expectations about speakers. I know who I preferred. With that in mind I now also assess my audience as well as interpreting the Bible. I start with Hebrews 5:12: "For though by this time you ought to be teachers, you need someone to teach you again the elementary truths of God's word all over again. You need milk and not solid food". This truth helps me in assessing where the young people are at, and what I can expect from them.

Teach basic truths in an interesting way

Most youth leaders serve teenagers from both inside and outside the church. Some of us also work across denominations and in more than one congregation. These factors mean it is vital to evaluate what the young people we are communicating with need. I find that teaching them basic truths can be difficult as it can offend some of them. But by blending basic truths with an engaging communication method you can actually give young people what they need.

My strategy

I developed a strategy which I named 'A5'. I have found it very effective when working with youth and always suggest it to my co-youth leaders. It helps meet expectations as well as maintain good relationships with young people. It stands for: Attention, Appreciation, Affection, Admiration and Aide Memoire.

We need to pay *attention* to how young people perceive things and what they feel about things; it is their time and they need to be given priority.

We should also *appreciate* their presence, their ideas and provide them with the opportunity to excel; let them say what is wrong or right, good or bad.

Our tender *affection* will empower them to express and overcome their fears and weaknesses; we all have our fears and weaknesses - so do they!

Our *admiration* of their tiniest efforts will encourage them and strengthen their faith in themselves; so let's encourage them.

And, most importantly, using an *aide memoire* helps them see we take their potential seriously. We make a note of our discussion with them and document it. This makes them feel that it's not just talk but will be acted on. I write the name, location, and key point and quote it to other young people as a reference.

I was never fond of going on leisure trips or picnics with young people, but I eventually figured out that it is the best place to overcome communication barriers and talk with young people away from the routine of life. Now at 'Rising Youth Forum' we plan a summer youth camp every year. In it we have short informal discussions and sessions using good resources, activities and fun! The best part is being able to share and communicate what we perhaps can't in a more formal environment.

7. Pastoral care of young people

Pastoral care works in a similar way to feedback for an organization or business; to be successful you need to properly evaluate what you are doing. You need all your activities pulling in the same direction. It is the same with pastoral care. It is very important that a youth leader checks that pastoral care is being carried out, not just whenever required, but regularly. Young people are fragile and need to be heard and given priority. It is a prime responsibility for the youth leader!

Your team of volunteers

Suniya my wife and I always recall Peter 2:9-10 in our treatment of young people. It says, "But you are a chosen generation, a royal priesthood, a holy nation, His own special people, that you may proclaim the praises of Him who called you out of darkness into His marvellous light. Who once were not a people but are now the people of God, who had not obtained mercy but now have obtained mercy". On the last Saturday of each month, and sometimes twice a month for breakfast, we spend time at our house with our team of volunteers with 'IMPACT – Pakistan' and 'Rising Youth Forum'. We have a great time sharing, reflecting and evaluating. Such an informal environment brings us close to each other and we get to know the issues we all tackle in our personal daily lives.

Man to man, woman to woman

In semi-urban and rural societies in Pakistan young people are dealt with on a gender basis. So Suniya and other female team members spend time with the girls and hear about their issues. In the same way the young men are given time with male team members so that they have privacy to be heard.

The wider church

Pastoral care is also the wider church's major responsibility, but here it is a weak area. Because of this, young people are neglected and are not involved in congregational activities, not given guidelines, nor are they given the opportunity to return back to church if they leave. So they become discouraged. Church leaders have forgotten this is part of their role. I once met with some workers in my church - the church officer and the gardener. They both shared personal issues with me. When I asked them to share this information with their church leaders the next time they visit their homes, they responded, "We have not seen any church leaders at our home for the last two years". I am not sure of the reasons for this, but if pastoral care was regularly undertaken then their issues would not have arisen. It would be a great source of help and comfort for those who are dealing with addictions, personal issues, family clashes, distress, as well as mental or physical health issues.

In Pakistan, many pastors and churches are lacking in this area. But, diligently done, it can help bring back many young souls and restore lost and stolen sheep.

8. Working with schools

In recent years, terrorist bombings and shootings at church buildings and schools has made the world aware of the sad situation in my country. Security today makes schools more like prisons, guarded by law enforcement agencies. This has a major psychological impact on children, their parents and teachers; instead of learning environments, schools are places of fear.

It is not only difficult for traditional Christian schools but also for military, government and major private school systems, and more specifically for girls and co-educational institutions. The Taliban [fundamentalist group] has sent threatening letters to a number of Christian schools telling them to be prepared for mass disaster. The government and law enforcement agencies have taken notice of this and tightened up the security of church buildings and schools. Yet even before the recent terror attacks, Pakistan was still a hard place for all religions - especially for Christians. Many hate Christians and those of other faiths. Nevertheless, Christian schools are a strong base for building character and decent human values into children and young people.

Since Christianity is based on a strong foundation, those of other faiths see Christian evangelism or openly Christian practices as a major threat. There is a long list of believers facing charges of blasphemy through the Pakistan Penal Code Section 295 A, B & C. Section 295C is used against Christians in the workplace, and many people have suffered greatly or been martyred.

My experience

In Pakistan, working with or getting into mainstream schools for youth ministry is not normal. However, the Church has a role and this is seen in annual Christmas or Easter programs and sometime in non-seasonal events. I previously worked in schools through *Gideons International*. The organisation visits teachers in schools to tell them what we do and also to distribute pocket-size New Testaments to those willing to receive them. It helped me become recognised by some young people from the church parishes we visit in our youth work. It gave me the opportunity to build on my connection with them and invite them to youth meetings.

My advice to youth leaders in Pakistan

First, encourage church leaders to focus on schools as part of their ministry or service to the community, and not as business or projects to make money.

Second, motivate parents to encourage schools in their community to help fulfil the spiritual needs of the children.

Third, liaise with church leaders and parents and form a special youth focused group in the school where the basic spiritual needs of young people are addressed.

My encouragement to youth leaders around the globe

You are in a unique position as regards schools! Do not view youth ministry as a profession or leisure pursuit; rather see it as an honor to be chosen to equip others and be used for God. Psalm 127:4-5 says this: "As arrows are in the hand of a mighty man so are the children of one's youth. Happy is the man that has his quiver full of them".

9. Leading a team and developing others

Leading and developing others should be a growing skill in a good youth leader. We all apply this differently depending on our own abilities and style. The benefit to young people makes it worth discussing since it is what youth leaders should be striving for from the start of their youth ministry.

Most of us understand that in order to lead others effectively we first need to learn to *serve*. After achieving this, if others are following us we can form a team. You cannot develop a team without having done the hard 'spade' work. It all depends on your dedication, willingness to serve, will power, patience, effort and experience in facing challenges, and by doing that we set an example and provide others with the opportunity to be prepared to deal with their own battles.

Hurdles and how to overcome them

In Pakistan, young people often face various types of resistance when starting a good work. This has to be dealt with patiently and also requires strong leaders. This resistance can be internal to the team, e.g. where there is a team member who lacks confidence or interest, or a teammate who does not like others on the team. It can also be external, e.g. when a parent confronts or discourages their teenager about their faith, or when the church leadership is fearful, or when the church has a weak foundation.

Being a youth leader I still face resistance to the work I am doing. I see how, for personal gain, church leaders pursue their own interests and in the process 'sacrifice' the young people. Large churches seem more prone to this as the leadership can lack leadership and vision, avoids delegating authority, fears sharing its knowledge, considers young people a threat, lacks trust and confidence in others' potential, or simply makes biased decisions. Youth leaders have to decide how they deal with these hurdles. They can respond negatively or positively.

In my early years in youth ministry I learned to respond positively to resistance rather than just reacting negatively. This helps avoid conflict and instead creates harmony and a long journey with the church and the young people. It is crucial that the youth leader sets an example that young people can follow.

Since part of your role as a youth leader is helping develop others, including young people, you sometimes get to know of the young people's abilities and hidden talents before other people do, sometimes even before the parents do. You need to discern which young people to really invest in, in order to empower them as future youth leaders. Because of this investment, 'Rising Youth Forum' now exists throughout Pakistan with a small number of volunteer workers who are self-motivated and can carry out the youth work on their own. They reach others to equip, empower, develop and encourage them in "Paying Back to the Community" which is our motto. In this way it helps show the youth to the whole church. My hope is that in time more young people will grow and their leadership will bring glory to God by reaching others!

10. Parents

In our society the local church is family and not an individual matter; the entire family attends the church service together. Ideally, children go to the children's ministry known as Sunday School and teenagers go to choir or youth group activities. This is the ideal perception of 'family' in our culture of life at the local church. Indeed, it is precisely what parents impart to us growing up.

So in Pakistan it is very important that a youth leader has access to parents. They have the major influence in decision making - what to do and what not to do, where to go or where not to. So we respect this and give heed to it.

Parents inside and outside of the church family

Working with parents who were, or are still are, involved in Church is a bit easier because they tend to completely support your efforts in youth work. Dealing with parents who are new to church or who once had a bitter experience is harder; it takes time to convince them about youth ministry and help them remember what it was like when they were a teenager.

In my local church I have a good relationship with parents. Sometimes parents bring their children and ask me to involve them in church; with others I have to share about the youth ministry to motivate the parents and encourage the young person.

The benefits of working with parents

It gives great pleasure seeing teens in your youth ministry reaching many others of their age. This only increases if parents recommend you to others as a great mentor or good resource person; they value your efforts and what you put into young people. Such appreciation is encouraging and helps you re-evaluate your scope for future ministry. Youth ministry helps parents and young people. By engaging parents we can evaluate how bonded a family is, how far apart the generations are, and what can be done to repair any damage. Putting things right also sets an example for young people for when they themselves are parents.

A handy way to remember what to do. Take AIM!
(Associate, Involve, Maintain)

- Associate with parents. You are an essential bridge for whole families. Let parents know what activities their young ones are doing, and let them get to know you so that they are comfortable with what you are doing and encourage young people to attend. This also helps create good family bonds.
- Involve parents. They can sometimes be a great support in helping with your youth ministry activities. It helps them see the value of youth ministry. Their involvement helps bridge the gap between the generations and brings out the hidden talents of both parents and young people.
- Maintain healthy relationships with parents. Parents have their own busy routines and priorities, so it's the responsibility of the youth leader to associate with and involve them regularly and not as a once a year event. Get their input frequently, seek their feedback. It will help develop trust and a sense of attachment.

11. You and senior church leaders

Youth leaders have to take the initiative in maintaining healthy relations with senior Church leadership and at the same time stay focused to the needs of the young people. I truly believe it is the youth leader's responsibility to maintain harmony with senior leaders if there seems to be conflict; this will help ensure the youth ministry runs well and is unaffected.

Don't be discouraged!

For the role of a youth leader you need to encourage yourself, have lots of patience, be humble and bear any resistance, keep yourself motivated, expand the leadership, and keep going regardless of who turns up.

You might have a helpful senior pastor who is encouraging and shares their own experience of growing a young ministry, e.g. initiation, energetic growth, sustained maturity and even demoralizing decline. Their understanding of the positives and negatives at each stage can boost your morale - a senior pastor who can give insight and help you carry out your ministry and believe that you can be fruitful! Yet a senior pastor may not be so encouraging.

Learning from senior leaders

In one parish in which I ministered, three priests came and went. All of them were older and very experienced and spent most of their time in congregational activities elsewhere. I learned a lot of things from them which were very useful in my future roles and ministry. I even quote their words now. Not all of my time was positive however. I tried to deal with it and learnt what I should and should not do. Here are the major positives and negatives, and what I learned.

Priest B was a friendly chap who united the church during a time of distress and developed a bond between young and old as well as between regular and seasonal members; but he showed favoritism and mistrust which drove many away from church.

Priest C was a good administrator and well-disciplined; but his discouraging perspective, especially of youth leaders, crushed people.

Priest D gave good structure and showed faith in young people to lead and take the initiative; however, his weak decision-making at times affected the young people negatively.

In summary

It is easy to assess and highlight weaknesses in others, but we cannot ignore our own flaws. We can learn not to repeat the mistakes of others but to apply good learning instead. We should not hold personal grudges or be biased towards particular leaders. We may need to repent from spiritual pride and reconcile with senior leaders and co-workers.

We should cultivate good qualities so they are reproduced in future generations of young leaders and the Church as whole. The Bible depicts a beautiful relationship between Paul and his apostolic representatives and the ministerial work carried out through them; we need to build that quality of relationship. We see the character of such leaders illustrated in 1 Timothy 3.

Chapter 8

Eero Haarala from Finland

My chapter is dedicated to my superb wife and to my core team in my ministry. I love you all.

1. My background and how I got into youth ministry

I come from Finland, a country between Russia and Sweden with a population of 5.5 million people. Apart from some large cities, the land is covered with thick pine forests, and thousands of lakes and islands. We Finns are known for things like the building of some of the world's largest cruise ships, mobile phones (Nokia), famous motor rallying and Formula 1 drivers, and cold weather. We are a very proud and stubborn people. There is no such thing as giving up! Finland has got a bloody history with Russia. For example, during World War II the Finnish army bravely defended the country from the far larger invading Soviet army, preventing it from making a decisive breakthrough into the heart of the country. Our capital city, Helsinki, was one of only three cities in Europe not invaded during World War II, the other two being London and Moscow.

My whole family lives in Finland and I have four brothers and three sisters. It is a big family! I spent my childhood in Oulainen, a small town near Oulu on the western edge of the country. My mother was a believer from the time she was expecting me. My father, who worked in a sawmill and the construction industry came to faith when I was 12 years old. My mother took me to the church, which was Pentecostal, so my roots are deeply embedded in the Pentecostal Church of Finland. The movement is not so charismatic as, say, in the U.S.A. This is because of the strong Lutheran Church influence over the denomination.

My mother took me to Sunday school and summer camps every year. At those camps I experienced God's love and presence several times. I accepted Christ into my life when I was 11 years of age and got baptised with water when I was 13. As a young person, another significant point was when I experienced the baptism of the Holy Spirit.

When I grew up, I went to agricultural school to learn about husbandry, machinery and farming. I graduated in agricultural professions in 1995 but I did not end up getting a job in the farming industry. Instead I worked as a mechanic in the Forest industry for over ten years. In Finland every adult male has to serve his country in the army or in the Civil Service; I served for 13 months in a hospital.

A few years after my time in the Civil Service I noticed a new girl called Maria at our church. She was so pretty and after a few months we got to know each other. Six months later we got engaged and the wedding took place a year after that. Our first child was born in 2001, a beautiful girl! Three years later we had a boy.

My route to becoming a youth pastor was a miracle. I was praying year after year that God would make His plan for my life clear. During my time working in the Forest industry it felt as if God did not see my desire and hunger. It was frustrating. I began working alongside the senior pastor in my home church as a trainee youth pastor. Then in 2004 I got a phone call from a church in Vantaa, which is right next to the capital, Helsinki.

The Pentecostal church there in the suburb of Korso had 380 members and they were looking for a youth pastor. They had got my name from another youth pastor who knew me. I was overwhelmed because I was about to start studying theology where I was. So, I took my family, sold our beautiful house and moved to Vantaa to begin youth work there. My start in ministry was hard and full of experiences which developed me significantly. I grew a lot and found my own identity in ministry and learned how to conduct myself properly.

My wife and I have now been at another church (Joensuu Pentecostal Church, East Finland) for about six years, but in total I have served for 15 years as a youth pastor. We have 120 young people in our current youth ministry.

2. Looking after your own soul

For all Christians there is one person on whom we have to focus. Even though we do ministry through the church we need consistent relationship with this person. It's all about Jesus! How I can build this relationship with Him? For me, praying daily and focusing on the Bible is the key to doing that. I don't have a structured plan for this any more as it something I do more naturally. Praying is like breathing or walking. It's important for me to keep my thoughts and my mind in prayer for the whole day. Sometimes I manage well and sometimes not so well. The point is that we listen for His voice through the day.

A plan

Sometimes it is not so quiet and things can interrupt concentrating on Jesus. That might be a crying child, a wife needing attention, people gossiping and stuff like that. You can get very irritated and frustrated. You want to punch a wall. During times like that I have felt I am not a good shepherd. So I find I need to get time on my own. I go into the woods or go for a walk alone. This helps create room to think and even to shout out my feelings to God. I use this time to plan my days. Even though I have a good routine for praying or reading I need to plan it out. It keeps me on track.

Working hours and family life

Working hours can be difficult in youth ministry, especially if you have small children. You work a lot of evenings and weekends whilst your family does the opposite! My wife goes to her job during the day and the children go to school during the daytime too. When do you see each other?! You have to keep your day off and not compromise. You may see somebody in the church struggling with their faith. They need your advice but you know your own family is expecting you for lunch or to take the children to the movies. These things used to upset me because when I began in youth ministry I often put others before my own family. But the most important 'mission field' is your own family. They need you!

Keep on learning

Reading the Bible and other good spiritual books helps keep the mind busy and on God. I find that to keep on learning is key to teaching others. You need new stuff in your mind all the time. There are at least two benefits from this. Firstly, you get refreshment for your own mind and soul. Secondly, you get new materials for teaching others. When you have preached tens or hundreds of times you have lots of good messages stored on your computer. It is OK to use old messages but don't do it too often. Keep them in your 'back pocket' for when you have more difficult times in your ministry. So exercise yourself in relationship with Jesus.

Make it a routine and a habit. This means that when hard times come you don't have to go such a long way to get close to God because it is something you do every day anyway.

Other youth pastors

For me is very important to have fellow youth pastors near me. With them I can share about my life, my successes and failures. They understand my challenges better than anybody else. Get somebody who you can tell your darkest secrets to, even maybe something that you don't immediately want to tell your spouse. You keep sinning, so you need Jesus and His forgiveness close to you. You're not made of steel!

3. Singleness, marriage and children

My story with girls goes back to when I was fifteen years old. I was in love with an amazing girl who was a little bit younger than I was. The relationship only lasted a few months. After that I dated several girls and I was quite reckless. This led to heartbreak for everyone concerned, me and the girls I got to know. In our church we did not have any good teaching about dating, so we had to work it all out ourselves. The only advice that I can remember was. "Keep God in your mind and your pants up"!

At my home, my parents had a conservative approach to marriage. They have been married for 40 years now and I respect them very much. But because as parents they had so many other things to deal with they did not say much about relationships. I had to find the right way on my own. You can imagine what kind of damage this caused me. I began to consume pornography. I think this is a huge problem today, greater than when I was in my youth.

I then tried to have better relationships with girls. A new girl called Maria started coming to our church but I did not pay attention to her because I was dating another girl at that time. I have since learned that Maria was sure that I was actually the right guy for her! So my future wife started to wait and pray. My relationship with her started in May 1998 at a youth gathering. We got to know each other that summer. Being apart for three months whilst she was in Greece for nursing training was a hard time for me; I was so in love with her. When she came back to Finland we got engaged and we married in August 1999.

I can't underline enough how important good teaching about dating and marriage is. Good examples of marriage are very important. In my ministry it is very important to show a biblical way to deal with the opposite sex. Sexuality is so important an area in young lives that we as pastors can't ignore it. I have been the pastor at several weddings. Every couple has to go through a few hours of preparation for marriage. In those conversations I teach them some key elements about marriage and raising children. Our example as parents, I hope, is important to all of them. When we live with one person for several years we have to deal with change; change as a couple and change as individuals. That woman or man you knew back in the early years of your marriage has partly gone. Your children grow up. If your marriage is based only on raising the kids you will be in great trouble after they are gone from your household. Ours have not left home yet, but I see my daughter (now age 15) is growing up very quickly! I encourage you to find private time with your spouse as much as possible.

4. Organising yourself and your ministry

At the start of my ministry as a youth pastor I was pretty disorganized. My working hours were ridiculous and I was not effective. My family suffered, so did the youth group, so did I. I had some kind of messiah syndrome going on. I didn't see the harm that my way of working was doing to the people closest to me.

God's call and other people

It took some years and strong guidance from my superiors and mentors to get me on track. I'm trying to keep my weekly working hours to 40 in a week, but often I do something like 60 in a week. This is a great challenge for me because I love my work so much and the people in it. God's voice is strong but sometimes I get confused about other human voices telling me what to do. This sometimes creates a kind of fuzz in my heart. When I learned to lead myself the right way I started to get my life more organized. I figured out that I have to keep my team close to me and avoid situations where I am alone with all the work. When I found the right co-leaders it made my work easier. I find I need to keep working at being organized. I have to search out better ways to do things all the time.

Sometimes this means I have to reflect hard about what I'm doing and what kind of leadership I'm providing. When you are going to be a pastor or volunteer in God's kingdom you need to know that you are called by God. Nobody can operate effectively in God's kingdom without the approval of our King and Master, our Lord Jesus. Most young youth pastors and those starting in God's work think about themselves too much. Everybody needs people around.

Transparency and fitting in with the vision of the church leadership

If you are not loyal to your own leaders it's hard to expect that kind of devotion from your volunteers, employees or co-workers. It's a known fact that those who are easy to lead are good leaders too. Do everything you can to make your own leader's life easier. Organize your work so well that you can make great efforts to help your leader. Sometimes we forget that the vision we carry must come under the vision of the overall church leadership. Youth pastors can forget that they are there to help make the church's vision come true in the youth ministry too. If the leadership has no clear vision it makes it hard in the youth ministry. If that is your situation then try to bring a positive influence to the wider church vision; don't try and do your own thing in the youth ministry.

Get advice

If you are not organized the very best way to get your own work organized is to ask a more experienced pastor to guide your way. In Finland we get mentors from outside of our own church. It is a good way to get an objective angle on how we are doing our youth ministry.

5. Keeping your evangelism edge sharp

In our ministry it's all about evangelism. How do we reach out to people in our home city? It's a huge question we ask all the time and it penetrates all that we do. First of all we keep training and encouraging our youth to be bold witnesses about Christ.

Practically, we do a few things for our young people. The Pentecostal movement has a wide range of training options in evangelism. These range from a few weekend seminars to doing two years of Bible school, studying theology and the practice of evangelism. Locally we do things each week. For example, every Friday evening we take our 'tea bus' to the main marketplace in our city. We give the youth gathered there the opportunity to have tea, coffee and bread during Friday celebrations in the bars and clubs from 9pm to 2am. Every Friday we encounter about 25-50 people. One benefit of this method is the low cost. It is an easy way to get close to youth who don't know Christ. In our church we have an education program for all who want to know about Christianity. This covers the basics of the faith. It's a little bit like the *Alpha* course but gives us an opportunity to give specific teaching in our denomination's theology. Even though Finland is a 'Christian' country, people do not know answers to basic questions about the faith. We have these courses in four different levels and this program runs throughout every year.

In youth ministry we also do a wide range of training in foreign missions; the *Kairos* course is one and offers different short term mission trips around the world. Our mission organization *Fida International* gives great support to our local churches in training and making contact around the world with different partners. So it's very easy to plan different kinds of missions trips with the youth. Every year we participate in a few mission or evangelism seminars around the country. Locally our church also gives opportunities to get training, experience and encouragement in sharing the gospel. Yet we still have a lot to do. Sometimes there are long periods of time when we see little result from all these efforts. All the time and money we spend does not benefit the church as we don't see the results instantly.

It is true that the most effective evangelists are the young people themselves, but especially young 14-16 year old girls. They have large social networks through school and their hobbies. They have a natural way to tell the gospel to their friends. We've seen great results from encouraging these girls. It's interesting to see how the boys appear after the girls. I am not sure why.

6. Communicating with youth

In my early days as a youth pastor my sermons were very short. It was frustrating because I had so much to say but not enough skill to do so. That's all history now and my sermons are longer (too long sometimes).

At the start I also did nct have a plan of what to teach. I soon realized that I needed a good plan to properly teach the youth grcup. The group was pretty small back then. With smaller groups, planning is even more important. First, I took a National Bible Association reading plan as a foundation for my teaching. The plan was to read the whcle Bible in one year. It is solic and good for small groups of youth. As the ministry grew larger, like 40 or 50 people on youth nights, we saw clearly how important it was to implement biblical principles in the daily lives of the young people. It is a big challenge to keep to solid theology when teaching kids. It's a risk if you only teach practical life skills because you can forget theology; you can lose contact with the Bible.

Larger groups

Now having been in youth ministry for over ten years, cur youth group has grown and also has many University students. We keep a good track of their needs and hopes and teach on things that are important to them. Topics that I keep on my teaching plan include marriage, sexuality, how to read and interpret the Bible, self confidence and identity in Christ.

Communicating with a large group of youth is almost impossible without a good system. In our church we have 120 people under 30 years of age. One pastor cannot know every young person. We have 11 small groups to help with this. I put in a lot of effort to coach and mentor young people who are small group leaders. As well as coaching them, we provide opportunities to participate in different kinds of seminars like the Global Leadership Summit (Willow Creek Association) or national youth leader gatherings. I have a good team of youth leaders to do this practical work with me. There are six of them and they are all young people.

Relationship and communication

Every Saturday night we have social time after youth meetings in a restaurant. By encouraging the young people in this way we also keep in contact with them. Social media like Facebook is also a good tool to get youth together to do cool things and to let them know what is coming up in next Saturday's teaching. Social media adds a lot of value. Teaching and contacting the youth go hand in hand. When you have good relationships and communicate well with youth, you can teach them more effectively.

7. Pastoral care of young people

Young people have to deal with several types of crisis: spiritual, social and others. Spiritual needs, in particular, need long term attention. The small groups in our church provide a place where everybody can share problems they are experiencing. Sometimes small group leaders need support and help with these different challenges and one of the main tools I use is personal guidance to solve people's personal problems. Counsel in spiritual things also gives a good opportunity to get to know young people. But it also means that I have to invest a lot of time in them. If you want to influence a young person's life, you have to spend a lot of time with them. Good times are coffee or lunch breaks during school or work, or after the sermon. This means that I have to invest some money in this kind of work. It is so true that the road to the human heart is through the stomach.

Trust and gender

Trust is the key factor in getting into a young person's heart. If you lose trust among youth you are in deep trouble. It is possible to get their trust back but it is very hard. This is where mentoring comes in. I think good pastoral mentoring needs spotless trust. Two people can help each other a lot, but someone who is more experienced can be a better mentor to someone less experienced. One principle of my counselling and mentoring is to do it man-to-man. I am very careful about this. If there is no woman to counsel the girls I work hard to get one or a few women to help me. If there is no woman to help me I keep looking. I make sure that my leaders know who I am mentoring or giving counsel to. Keep your life pure and do not give opportunities for anyone to blame you in these relationships with youth.

Parents and local government

When you are dealing with young people, especially those who are not adults, keep parents well informed. Sometimes you may have problems with a young person and the parents are a big part of the problem.

In Finland the government is very involved in child care. When parents are violent or a child's life or health is in danger we have to inform the authorities. These kinds of problems are pretty rare, but possible. With the local authorities we make plans to help the whole family get through difficult situations.

Spiritual abuse and leadership

Sometimes those in leadership spiritually abuse young people. It is very tricky for a pastor to try and repair the damage. Healthy relationships in the church give a good base for spiritual life so it is very important to nourish this important part of young people's lives. As leaders and pastors we have a great responsibility in our work with youth. We are to be examples of a Godly life. We lead by our lives and are accountable for our teaching as well. Keep track of what you are teaching and make sure you practise what you preach.

8. Working with schools

Finnish society has strong Lutheran roots going back centuries. So the Pentecostal movement that came later is partly based on Lutheran spirituality; we therefore have the most Lutheran-Pentecostals in the world! Lutherans make up around 83% of the population in our country. Even with so many people identifying themselves as Lutheran and Christian there is a lack of faith in our country. Many Lutherans do not participate actively in church life. Most people go to church services for baptisms, weddings and funerals. In schools children are educated about various denominations and faiths. It is possible to have classes in Islam, Buddhism, Krishna or minor denominations in Christianity. Finnish education upholds the human right of freedom of religion/belief.

For example, if you have three students in a registered denomination, you have the right to ask the religious education department in their school and town councils to arrange religious education to suit their choice of denomination. So we teach religion in our schools and the situation in our country is good in that young people are taught about religion. It forms a good basis of understanding. It gives good tools for almost every part of life and helps give young people a good future. But in bigger cities the trend is to avoid doing this if possible. In such cases it is hard to get pastors and other ministers into these schools.

Pentecostals and my work into schools

In Finland the Pentecostal Church has done excellent work in the school system for almost 40 years. We have regions where there are regional school pastors to help local churches. Only 1% of Finns are Pentecostals, yet almost every school in our country gets information about our denomination every few years. Many local churches keep up good relationships with schools and take religious education lessons in schools. My own work in schools happens once a year. In our city there are 10,000 students in Grades 1-9 (ages 7-16). I do my work with 7th to 9th graders and in high schools. When I came to Joensuu, my home city, I went to see the head of the education sector and told him what I wanted to do in schools. After that I went to meet every school principal in our city. Some schools said that they didn't need our services at all; others welcomed us with open arms. Those school principals who don't want us coming in say that the Lutheran church does enough. Lutherans have good contact with the young people because when pupils are aged 15 they are invited to a baptism/communion course. Almost 75% of all students do this course to confirm their baptism as a child!

When I go into a school I have to make sure for myself what the rules are. You cannot force religion on anyone. You can't make pupils pray or tell them that they have to believe in Jesus. There are boundaries that you can't get over. Trust is everything with schools. In my ministry it is very important to get along with schools. It keeps me fresh when I can go to a class and see how youth are outside the church. It is good when we have effective relationships with key people such as teachers and school principals in our city. Get God's Word into schools; it never comes back empty.

9. Leading a team and developing others

I have been leading teams of volunteers for about ten years. It has been hard, but rewarding at the same time. I find that leading a team of volunteers is the best and most interesting part of my ministry. Establishing a great team is an ongoing process and it is never finished. When a team is working effectively there is power and motivation. Every member makes a lot of effort, everything works well and any problems seem small. We all wish it was like this all the time!

Challenges

It is challenging because people move on and the team can change a lot. Sometimes it is frustrating because you will have been investing a lot of time in one person and after a short period of time they leave. Building a solid long term team in youth ministry is difficult, seemingly impossible. In a team there can be conflict, frustration and a lack of motivation; things are not always 'spiritual'. People can criticise each other when the ministry has some issues. Teams can even fall apart because of these things. As the youth pastor or team leader you take the most criticism.

The elders or a church board may also blame the lead pastor or senior leader for problems. This is pretty understandable. As team leaders we have responsibility for our teams and the people in them. Most of the time when a team is not working the answer lies with the leader who is in charge; it is your responsibility as the team leader to fix it. Most of the time, as a youth pastor I have to make sure that there is always a 'Plan B' if someone suddenly leaves. This means that I have to know everything in our youth work so that when someone leaves I can deal with any problems that immediately arise. There are always people needing mentored or helped in their specific task in the youth work. Yet despite the difficulties it is very rewarding!

Benefits

One of the myths in youth ministry is that it is simply a short term thing. Too many youth pastors think youth ministry is simply a stepping stone to become a lead pastor in a church. Working with young people and teams of leaders is one of the most challenging areas in the life of a church! The youth pastor's role needs a lot of skill, more than many other tasks in a church. Doing long term youth ministry gives you a wide range of experience in God's kingdom. I want to encourage every youth pastor to have a long career in youth ministry. Young people need long term relationships with adults. It is so cool to work years and years with the same people, see them grow in God and mature into adulthood!

10. Parents

After more than ten years of youth ministry I get on well with parents; they are more vital to me than ever. Parents can be a great asset to your work in your ministry. It makes things easier when you maintain contact and have a good relationship with them; after all, it is a great responsibility to be in charge of their children when they are at youth activities.

Families are key to church growth. When parents get good support from the church in their responsibilities they are more likely to bring their children to church. Today there is less community and fewer relatives nearby, so parents are often on their own with the challenge of bringing up their children. This makes the youth pastor's role in the teen's life very important. You can't focus on spirituality only, you have to know what kind of challenges they have in their life, for example: studies, relationships, self-esteem problems and so on. There is a bundle of issues where we youth leaders are in a key position to help teenagers through difficulties in life.

Sometimes, of course, things can go wrong. Parents can object to their child attending church or youth group. Good preparation for these situations is important. When a teenager from a non-Christian home comes to your group make sure that you tell the parents somehow what it is that your youth ministry does. If you hide things from parents you will suffer for it later.

In Finland, the law forces us to keep these things in order. For example, it is difficult to take underage teenagers on youth activities without getting permission from their parents. In fact, we must get their signature first. This forces youth pastors to maintain good contact with parents. Finnish society pushes hard to make sure churches protect children in their community. This is good because there will always be people and leaders who will take advantage of young people if they have the opportunity. The Finnish Pentecostal Church has guidelines and safety procedures to make sure young people in our youth ministries are kept safe. There are guidelines about running camps, counseling youth, and who can and cannot work with children. Every church has to have good policies and procedures in place to prevent child abuse. All this gives credibility to our work and ministry. Because we are open about what we are doing it makes things much easier.

It is very inspiring to deal with youth and their families. When you see good results from working with them it is encouraging for your life and ministry. Everybody needs encouragement, so do you! If you want results in youth ministry then make sure that as part of your calling you honor parents.

11. You and senior church leaders

When I started my first youth ministry role in my home town I soon learned a few things. One was that I needed to understand that I was not just going to spend time pastoring young people. I struggled sometimes with my senior pastor because he wanted me to spend time with older people in the church! "What is the point of that?", I thought. I asked my church leader and I got a clear answer: "They pray for you and help pay your salary, so honor them and spend some with them". So I took some time to develop relationships with older people in the church. The effect on the youth ministry was huge. When some big issues came up in my ministry I then had lots of support from them. The church board and elders also listened to me more carefully and took my opinions seriously. Lots of people prayed for me and my family. On one church day trip for older people I told them all about the youth ministry, e.g. the challenges, how many young people came to faith in the last few months, etc. One of the cool things is the great wisdom these older people had to offer me. I listened carefully to what they said and never mentioned any lack of knowledge they might have about modern youth culture, nor did I try to convince them that youth ministry is superior. So overall I learned this: be humble towards older people in your church.

What about the church leadership team or church board/elders?

You're not responsible to the youth for your leadership. They can't fire you, but church leaders can. This is very important to understand. Don't lose the trust of your leaders! If you want to serve in the best way then keep up good relationships with your leaders. Maintain good contact with them; this will help keep your spirit in good condition. A young person can cause problems if they are not happy with you, or some counsel or guidance they have had. But young people come and go; they move on. If you have a trusting relationship with your leaders and other workers in your church then you have a better chance of succeeding in your ministry despite these difficulties.

Don't build a church within a church

There is great trap if you are called into youth ministry. Occasionally it is tempting to build your own ministry and vision. This is wrong and does not help build God's Kingdom. I've been there a few times! Whenever I started to build my own vision instead of serving God's or the church's I failed in my ministry. So don't build a 'church inside the church'. Your youth ministry is not yours, it's God's and part of the church's ministry. Your task is to help build the church through the youth ministry. Attend board meetings and listen carefully to what kind of plans your church has, what the big picture is. Make sure your efforts are in line with the overall vision of the church. Don't pull it in your own direction. Be loyal to God and to your leaders.

Chapter 9
Gary McCusker from the U.S.A.

My chapter is dedicated to Debi, my beloved wife and partner in ministry for over forty years.

1. My background and how I got into youth ministry

Similar to a lot of American kids growing up with parents serving in the military, I spent my early years living in a variety of countries like Germany and Scotland - my mother's home country - and different parts of America, including California. As a teenager, I attended a large public high school and that's where Jesus revealed himself to me through the ministry of Young Life, a para-church youth ministry in the USA. My life was transformed and I grew from an insecure adolescent into an engaged relational evangelist to my friends at school.

After high school, I attended college in Idaho, USA, where I soon met Debi, the love of my life, and we were married a few years later. Together we returned to California to finish college, and found a strong church to help us both. I pursued my passion for reaching young people for Christ through coaching athletics, which led to a connection with the schools ministry of Youth for Christ. Debi and I decided to forego our respective careers and instead join Youth for Christ full time as missionaries in California, responding to God's call to reach young people with the Gospel. We spent seven years there and God blessed us with two children.

With another child soon to arrive God opened a door for us to work with youth in military families based in Germany. It was a joint venture with Young Life and Youth for Christ, working with both Catholic and Protestant chaplains as the only full-time spiritual leaders in a military community based in Europe. Our children attended German schools and thrived as third culture and missionary kids. It was a very special season of our lives. Aside from various leadership roles my wife and I had working alongside chaplains and military leaders we traveled extensively around Europe, both in ministry but also on holiday/vacation.

After nine years Debi and I both clearly sensed God calling us back to the USA where I took time off from Youth for Christ to earn a Master's Degree in Biblical Counseling at Colorado Christian University. We started attending Parker Evangelical Presbyterian Church (PEPC), Colorado, USA, where we had some connections, and that community quickly grew to be our spiritual home and family as we acclimated back into USA culture. When the youth pastor there resigned I volunteered to be the interim replacement out of concern that my own teenage children would not have a church home to grow in as disciples of Jesus. In 1999, I left Youth for Christ to become the full time Youth Pastor, serving until my 50th birthday. Serving at the same church and in the same community for over twenty years, although not devoid of hardship, has taught me the secret of longevity in youth ministry: one must not be a soloist but a team builder to reach many more young people.

Twenty-one years later I am still at the same church. I now serve as the Associate Family Life Pastor overseeing youth leaders, encouraging husbands, and coaching baseball. My wife Debi serves as the Vice President of Operations for Youth for Christ, USA. We thoroughly enjoy the place God has us as we strive to empower and equip younger leaders. After a long process of study I was ordained as a pastor in 2012. My wife and I have a wonderful relationship with each of our adult children. We now have one grandchild! We enjoy spending our free time outdoors, as we love to hike, snowshoe, golf and travel as a couple. God is so good!

2. Looking after your own soul

I am thankful for the mentors whom God has provided for me along the way for almost forty years. The consistent message from each of them has been this: "You cannot pass on what you do not have." They regularly confirmed that my relationship with Jesus had always to be my first love and priority.

The times I felt most ineffective and overwhelmed was when I permitted my spiritual disciplines to waver. The times I felt the Holy Spirit use me most powerfully was when it was an outpouring of His love and faithfulness in me. I learned that for me to have a life-giving relationship with Jesus Christ I needed to journal, i.e. write out my prayers, burdens and praises. This discipline helped me to clear my mind and heart and tune into the passages of Scripture I would be reading, or prayers that I would be speaking. Some other tools that have been instrumental were praying the A.C.T.S. system, starting with Adoration (Praising God), Confession

(Repenting of my sins), Thanksgiving (Keeping an attitude of gratitude) and Supplication (Petitions for people, needs or concerns for my life or for others).

For many years, I felt that Oswald Chambers was my pastor as I would read the daily devotional book, *My Utmost for His Highest*. Although he died over a hundred years ago it seemed like his writings were connecting me intimately with God each and every day. I also looked for ways to appease my spiritual hunger by searching for resources to grow deeper in my knowledge of Scripture. Often I would listen to sermons of people whom I respected and knew were gifted teachers of God's Word. God has always impressed upon me that He is the one who called me and that He would be the one to sustain my soul and fuel my calling to reach young people with His glorious Gospel.

The main source for someone with my particular temperament and personality to sustain their spiritual health is through authentic and accountable relationships. These relationships needed to be with people who care more about me as their brother in Christ than what I did as a minister of the Gospel. I have thrived spiritually when I have met regularly with a group of like-minded men, or men and women. It has been life-giving interaction with fellow believers who knew me and would encourage and challenge me to seek Jesus first, and then remind me that ministry will naturally follow. I truly believe I am still experiencing effective and fulfilling ministry at the present time as a result of the many faithful mentors in Christ who have prayerfully walked with me through the years.

3. Singleness, marriage and children

Debi and I were married while still students in college, which was before we started our professional ministry, so in terms of work I have known only youth ministry as a married man, and then as a father. Debi and I began in Youth for Christ, first as part-time leaders then as full-time staff members upon graduation. From the beginning we felt the call to ministry as a couple, and it was our focus which often consumed every area of our lives. Fortunately, God provided some ministry staff couples who modelled for us how to protect and prioritise our marriage in light of the demands of youth ministry.

My primary responsibilities were to provide leadership for students, volunteers, parents and represent the organization, whereas Debi was my key women's staff person. She ministered primarily to female students but also oversaw the operations of the ministry with her training, spiritual gifts, administrative and financial skills. At every Youth for Christ regional or national gathering, the leaders provided valuable resources that spoke to the importance of maintaining a healthy and intimate marriage. Their admonitions came at the appropriate time as to avoid the many pitfalls of making the ministry more important than our marriage or family. I am grateful for a wife that felt the call to ministry to the same level that God called me. She was the one who often sent signal flares over the bow of our marriage that forewarned me that I was becoming too consumed with everyone else's needs and not remembering hers and our children's. I know it may have seemed to Debi that I was not responding initially but God always seemed to grasp my attention and to correct my misguided enthusiasm and later to refocus my priorities. As I reflect, God honoured those adjustments and breathed life into the ministry without my need to do it all. What a relief to acknowledge God's sovereignty and freedom which provided a catalyst for ministry, rather than developing a messiah complex, where I felt it was all my responsibility to make ministry happen!

When we began full-time ministry, we joyfully discovered that we would be expecting our first child. Although we were very poor financially and a bit overwhelmed with the tasks of our ministry responsibilities, in retrospect it was a blessing to start our ministry full-time balancing all of these new roles. We needed to be attentive and nurturing parents as well as loving spouses to one another. Even though our lives were very fruitful we stumbled at times, but the grace of our Lord Jesus Christ, a close knit ministry team (people around us who became adoptive aunts and uncles) and students that became a part of our lives, all made for a rich experience as a young family.

Although I would often find myself becoming overextended by giving everything to the ministry, my faithful wife's love, support, and the joy of being a father kept me close to home. The wisdom of my mentors reminding me to keep God first, family second and ministry third has been a recipe for longevity in ministry. This longevity has been the greatest measure of effective evangelism and discipleship of students for almost four decades. A healthy and intimate marriage, and close relationship with our now adult children, has been the greatest witness to the power of the Gospel in our lives. I am truly a blessed husband, father, grandfather and a thankful servant of our Lord Jesus Christ.

4. Organizing yourself and your ministry

My family instilled within me a strong work ethic but organisational skills have always been an issue for me. I am married to a highly organised and systematic woman who has given me insights into how best to complement my strong relational skills and ministry focus. One of the simple ways that Debi has influenced me is to make lists of my duties and responsibilities. I learned from my administrative directors and staff that I should permit them to assist me in areas where I am not gifted organisationally. I learned quickly to use other staff members' systems, outlines, processes and to make them my own.

I also realised as I worked on various teams that God has given us all different spiritual gifts, abilities, passions and experiences. I learned from tests like the Myers-Briggs Type Indicator, that as a 'compassionate leader' I desire to identify and affirm the gifts of others as well as affirm my own spiritual gifts. It was critical to be honest with myself and my colleagues that along with one's strengths we also have limitations and weaknesses. The awareness of my inadequacies did not excuse me from being disorganised but it did make me conscious that I needed to get others to complement my shortcomings administratively.

One tool I have used to assist in these inadequacies is having a notebook or a diary with me all the time so I can write down important facts and dates or promises that I would make. Many today prefer to use a smartphone or similar, but it is still good, even in our modern society, for people to see you noting down a task, duty or an idea. Another tool has been writing my weekly schedule and giving it to my wife, administrative and ministry staff to better communicate my plans, appointments, time with family, planning times and office work. Perception always becomes reality if people know that you are attempting to use your time wisely, and they become stronger advocates of your calling and ministry.

During my early ministry one of my Youth for Christ mentors taught me that if my words are not reliable than I am not reliable. This motto has been embedded in my heart, mind and soul for most of my life. If I am not responsible, it reflects on my Lord and Savior Jesus Christ, whom I am endeavoring to share with students and their families. This nugget of wisdom from my dear friend comes directly from Jesus' teaching in the Sermon on the Mount as recorded in Matthew 5:37, "All you need to say is simply 'Yes' or 'No'; anything beyond this comes from the evil one." In other words, Jesus exhorts us to be completely honest in our verbal interactions with others.

In conclusion, my main suggestion for effective and long lasting ministry if someone has a deficit in organizational and administrative skills (like myself), is to invite others with those gifts to be a part of your team and vision to reach students with the Gospel. Ultimately, the ministry will flourish and everyone will be blessed by the spiritual fruit it accomplishes for God's Kingdom.

5. Keeping your evangelism edge sharp

Since I came to faith in Jesus Christ as a fifteen year old, through the outreach of school friends and acquaintances, it was natural for me to integrate evangelism into the church as an integral part of youth ministry. Evangelism is common ground for me personally and it has been part of any youth ministry teams I have led.

For me, evangelism is all about: 1) blending my relationship with others through life's everyday interactions, 2) my commitment to God through personal communion with Jesus Christ, and 3) how we prayerfully introduce the two of them to each other. Our colleagues and partners in ministry at Youth for Christ call this type of ministry *Three Story Evangelism:* Their story, Your story, and God's story.

I have been deeply influenced by the evangelistic ministries of Youth for Christ and Young Life and their relational approach that seems to stem from the advice Paul gives to us in 1 Corinthians 9:22 & 23, "that we might find common ground with the non-believer and become all things to all people so that we may save some." During my forty years of ministry, those areas of common ground have included skiing, surfing, biking, rafting, mountain climbing, traveling, coaching sports, mission trips and serving those who have experienced various types of loss. Each of these areas represents at least two things: one, it is in a non-threatening environment that builds authentic friendships; two, it is learning together a new skill or attempting a new experience. These interactions create fertile and common ground to share our most important relationships, which for me included my personal faith in Jesus Christ, which I could then share on a conversational and relational level.

So I have discovered that the less confrontational the evangelistic method is, the more open to the truth most people, especially teenagers, are to respond to a personal relationship with Jesus. Of course, the effectiveness of these long-term evangelistic efforts is based upon the quality of the relationship with the individuals you desire to reach with the Gospel. These kinds of relationships take more time but usually result in more quality professions of faith in Christ.

My experience has been that when students experience the impact of their prayers and God blesses their efforts to reach their friends with the Gospel, it transforms them and their faith in a profound manner. It often becomes a contagious movement when they witness their prayers being answered in seeing lives dramatically changed when their friends genuinely encounter Jesus.

When evangelism becomes merely a strategy or gimmick, my experience is that a youth ministry loses its effectiveness in reaching those close to your core young people. The attractiveness of Jesus in the Gospels is His love, compassion, acceptance and kindness to those who are lost, hurting, rejected and wounded. As a youth pastor or youth leader, our students must observe this love in action as we reach out to those in our world. The saying that things are 'more caught than taught' is true, and this is especially true when it comes to evangelism.

6. Communicating with youth

I believe one of the vital keys to effectively communicating with youth, is first to win their trust and respect. Once that essential foundation is laid, my experience is that most students will give their youth pastor their attention, interest, hearts and minds. The saying, "Young people do not care how much you know until they know how much you care" has been a cornerstone to effective communication with the young people I have taught, mentored or coached for the previous four decades.

The founder of Young Life, Jim Rayburn said, "It is a sin to bore a kid." This quote has influenced me every time I have led a small group or have spoken to hundreds of students at a camp, or a student leadership conference. It is important to know your audience, their age, attention span, spiritual and emotional maturity and then craft your message to best communicate the Gospel or biblical truth to them. Since Jesus used parables to communicate truths to those who were attentive to his message, it is logical to present stories that are relevant to the youth we are hoping to connect to Christ and to the church. I have found that sharing personal stories that reveal my own struggle and need for Jesus' wisdom and healing touch, quickly creates a level ground between the audience and myself. I think that personal stories combined with well-told illustrations are critical to making communication come alive with young people. I believe that humor, especially if we can laugh at ourselves, is a wonderful conduit for sharing God's golden nuggets of wisdom, grace and love from the Scriptures. Any time a youth pastor can take a Bible passage and contextualize it with a present day situation it can bring the message even more alive and applicable.

Since youth ministry is all encompassing, I discovered that I did not need to have original ideas every time I spoke to or taught young people, as long as I was willing to give others credit for their material. At the present time we have many gifted youth communicators who have made their materials available to be used by busy youth leaders. My suggestion is to never read directly from a book or resource manual but to transcribe it into your own words or teaching style in order that your students connect with the material.

When it is time for Bible teaching or Bible studies, it is critical to have your students investigate the Scriptures for themselves and then guide them on how to use God's Word effectively. As a result, they can spiritually enrich their own lives as well as teach others. Another key to being a successful communicator is to be a motivated learner alongside your students. It is vital to always be a few steps ahead of them in your learning of spiritual truths and ideas because we cannot teach what we do not know. If we model teaching, then we are modeling growth as a life-long disciple of Jesus Christ. A final key is that we need to introduce our youth to like-minded teachers and communicators who are either volunteers or fellow youth leaders who will complement and support the discipleship process of our youth.

7. Pastoral care of young people

In my twenties I ministered in certain pastoral care situations much differently to how I responded to them in my forties, but my core principles have remained the same. The first principle is that the ministry of 'presence' and, more often, the ministry of 'silence' are vital to effectively ministering to individuals and families in any kind of crisis. The second principle is to know your limitations and how and when to speak effectively into a critical situation. And the third principle is to have a resource team of professionals at your disposal to walk alongside you as you minister to those in need. It is important that we do not appear to be an authority in an area in which we have little training or competence concerning an area of care, such as: the death of a loved one, an actual or attempted suicide, mental illness, addiction to a substance or a behavioral problem. Therefore, if you are a trusted person to the individual or a family, your connection to a credible resource could be a life changing link to those to whom you are ministering. Often the tendency when we are faced with difficult situations is to avoid or dismiss our value. This is the time when we need to gently make ourselves visible and available to love, serve, pray and encourage those experiencing unusual circumstances.

I remember vividly a summer night over ten years ago when I was awakened by a telephone call from a volunteer staff member. He was weeping uncontrollably and it was difficult to understand what he was trying to communicate. I was finally able to understand that his little brother, who was in my small group, along with two students and an adult were killed in a car accident earlier that evening. That night and the next day I found myself at the hospital where the boys were admitted and then at their school the next morning where the community was in shock over the horror of what had taken place. In the midst of my own grief for the loss of the student and for his family, who were best known to me, I was drawn into the grief of the other four families of the students, especially for the driver who had survived the accident and was still hospitalized. The next week, I was a key point of pastoral support to each of the families, ministering at all three funeral services and then at a combined memorial service at their high school. It was broadcast through local and national networks, with reporters wanting to know more of the details of what truly transpired the night of the accident that rippled grief through our community. I was grateful for our church staff and other youth leaders within our community that shielded me from media distractions. It freed me to give hundreds of hugs, speak gently into the ears and hearts of devastated family members and friends of the young men. During that week I experienced supernatural strength and energy for I was aware that thousands of people in our community and around the world were praying for the families, and specifically for me, to share the healing love of Christ to those closest to the tragedy.

At the funeral of Michael, the young man from our church, I made a promise to remember him and his friends through an annual flag-football tournament which has become a fundraiser for student mission scholarships. Over ten years later, it is a time and place of healing and reconnection for the families and close friends forever impacted by this tragedy. The love, truth and hope of the Gospel continues to flow from the outreach in which the Christian community responded gently, kindly and wisely to those who came from a myriad of religious backgrounds. The Holy Spirit guided my steps and my heart in those tumultuous moments of being a youth pastor placed in the middle of extreme brokenness. On each anniversary of this event, I continue to receive heartfelt messages of appreciation for being a minister of presence and a minister of silence in their lives.

8. Working with schools

The student culture in which we minister is greatly influenced by at least three primary environments: the home, the school and the media. When a young person's family is involved in church, we can often have access to their home life. If we want to truly know our student's world, having an entry point into their schools is a tremendous asset to discovering their goals, aspirations and values, along with the hope of communicating the Gospel.

In the United States of America navigating the issue of the separation of church and state, in order to gain entry to a school, can be a cumbersome but not impossible feat. In other areas of the world, like in Europe where my children received their early educational learning, they have religious classes often taught by local clergy or a ministry person. This is not the usual procedure in the United States, but in over three decades of student ministry there has been only one year where I was denied access to my students on their respective campuses. I learned quickly, through the counsel of other youth leaders, to make myself available on a voluntary basis which opened up numerous windows of opportunity.

One of the first questions after meeting a school principal or headmaster was, "How may I serve you to better educate and meet the needs of your student body?" At first they may have been apprehensive, but when they made a suggestion I was quick to respond affirmatively and then to serve in a quality manner to assist in meeting those needs. Those requests varied from chaperoning at a school activity, providing a free lunch, bringing coffee and treats to a teacher's in-service training day or organizing and participating in a campus trash clean-up event. Whenever we are working with those outside the church, we must gain their confidence that we are not there to violate their trust. Most administrators are concerned that we will cause more trouble than we are worth by violating their openness and proselytizing their students on campus. Often their fear, mostly due to previous violations of trust, is that we have a hidden agenda that will ultimately create conflicts with the overall community that they serve. When we are given an opportunity to partner, we need to honor their established guidelines, and give wholehearted service to the administration, staff and students.

I also offered my services as an experienced coach or referee to meet a responsibility they might not have been able to fill among their staff members. These service opportunities placed me in close proximity to the students of my church, which only built a stronger connection and respect with them. They soon realized that I was concerned about their everyday world and life outside of their church involvement. There are other ways to serve: sign up as a substitute teacher, volunteer with a skill that you can offer such as debating, photography, drama or tutoring. I have discovered that walking through the door of a school, as a welcomed volunteer or visitor, has often opened doors into the hearts and lives of my students as well as acceptance by many of their non-believing classmates.

9. Leading a team and developing others

My extensive experience as an athletics coach has mirrored and complemented my youth ministry career. This has been the key to success for me in both athletics and ministry as I strongly emphasize the concept of 'team.' An effective youth ministry model is not personality-centric but a living picture of I Corinthians, chapter 12, describing the Body of Christ in action. A team of leaders is one where they work in harmony to use their gifts to effectively maximize the influence of the Gospel message to students.

Youth ministry is much more enjoyable when you have a strong team of volunteers who love Jesus, desire to be together and are passionate about ministering to young people. It all sounds of the highest level but it requires a lot of work and focus for the leader to arrive at that optimal place of having a solid ministry team. First, you should to be willing to invest in volunteer leaders through a robust application and interview process that establishes the ground rules and commitment level before a leader ever connects with students. The benefit of having this approach to team ministry is that when students realize the diversity of gender, age, personalities, spiritual maturity and gifts, they are more likely to commit themselves to a leader and there is a greater probability of a leader-student connection. Second, the youth leader should be willing to share his or her time, training and resources with others rather than focus strictly on his or her own personal growth and development. This becomes an issue of control for the youth leader when they trust that the team approach is more effective than what one skilled youth leader can accomplish on their own.

It takes time and energy to include others in your life's passion and ministry team. Overall, I found it to be more effective and enjoyable as you witness their growth and positive influence as youth ministry leaders. During my time of emphasizing this approach I have also had leaders who have abused their position of authority or used my trust to attain their own agenda. This resulted in divisiveness and even destructive and harmful behavior towards students. When these rare instances occurred, my tendency was to regain control and limit others from becoming a part of our ministry team. Fortunately, from those adverse situations I learned how to better recruit, screen and train leaders so that it might not happen again. Ultimately, through these kinds of experiences, I became a better shepherd of the flock of students that God had entrusted to me for the purpose of more effective ministry and discipleship.

One of the intrinsic results and rewards from this kind of team ministry model is that one of the volunteer leaders recognizes God's call to pursue a full time student ministry position. When this occurs, it not only fulfils the volunteer leader's call but fulfils the call of the youth pastor to "go make disciples" (Matthew 28:19 & 20).

10. Parents

Fortunately, we began full time youth ministry while my wife, Debi, was pregnant with our first child. At that time we were made keenly aware of the extended ministry that we would have with parents through their children. It soon became very evident that we were working with parents' treasures - their children. Embracing this reality has always been a strength of our ministry to young people and overall we have benefited greatly from our partnership with parents.

Parents are as varied as the students whom we serve: some are single parents, step-parents, non-believing parents, parents who are overbearing, absent parents, young and old parents, grandparents, parents who are staff members, elders or deacons, but the one key value to establish with all parents is trust. Parents need to know that you can be trusted with their child or children at all times. Here are a few nuggets of wisdom that I have gained to help build a level of trust with parents which allowed me, as a youth worker, to fully engage with their children.

First, it is critical to communicate with them through whatever media is available and popular at that time. They need to know what you are doing, what your intentions are, places you are going and how to best contact the leader if needed. It is important to communicate any information that will reinforce to them that you are transparent and a trusted adult when it pertains to their child or children. Second, they need to see that you are true to your word, that your 'yes is yes' and your 'no is no.' Parents must know that you will never turn their child against them, even if you disagree with their parenting style or disciplinary actions. Third, it is important to communicate that you are always available to them for clarification, questions and insights. Lastly, they need to know that you are willing to come alongside them to enhance their relationship with their child, especially in those problematic times that we all know will occur during those adolescent years.

Early in our ministry, when having a place to meet was an issue, we would meet in the homes of students and rotate locations each month. This provided a natural relational bridge with parents as they would host a large crowd of young people. They witnessed first-hand our genuine love for God and for young people from the moment we entered their homes. We realized very quickly that their advocacy was an enthusiastic endorsement to other parents, who then would readily open their homes and resources for ministry opportunities and meeting locations.

As our children reached their teenage years, our ministry to our students' parents only increased as they knew we were facing some of the same kinds of challenges in rearing teenagers. Often, God opened many doors to introduce non-believing parents to Jesus Christ. We often watched as a whole household become spiritually transformed through their children's involvement.

In some of the locations that we ministered, we did not have the availability of volunteer youth leaders but we found that parents were available as volunteers. They already had a vested interest and could be used as part of our leadership team. We would ask the students' permission prior to the invitation and reassure them, if needed, that we would create a healthy distance between them and their parents.

Some youth leaders find that parents can be rather annoying and even a burden, whereas I am thankful for our positive experiences from the time we first began ministering to young people. I strongly suggest that every youth leader has a parent support group, a parent council or a structured opportunity for parents to be involved and become a viable resource in reaching their youth for Christ. Remember they are the ones who literally have 'skin in the game' for your ministry to be successful.

11. You and senior church leaders

My youth ministry experience in a military community taught me to never surprise the leadership. The key was to communicate everything concerning what you were hoping to do with the youth, what you were doing with them at the time, and then to report on the results as soon as possible. I learned the skill of asking permission and reporting as quickly and clearly as possible - this was a non-negotiable no matter what the outcome. I became keenly aware that I was never to surprise them as that might be my last opportunity to serve that Chief of Chaplains or Commander. The saying, "I'll ask forgiveness rather than permission" was not going to go very far in this particular ministry environment! I believe this training laid the groundwork for my ability to have quality relationships with the senior leadership I have served during most of my ministry career.

Our primary responsibility is to faithfully serve God with all that we do while ministering to young people, but our allegiance to our senior pastor or senior advisor is a close second. If we are supportive and faithful to our leadership, he or she for the most part will make our ministry efforts so much easier. In turn they will be better advocates for resources that are needed for youth ministry to thrive. Again, I believe this is one of the principles which has been instrumental in my youth ministry fulfillment and success. Most senior staff know that finding a youth leader who connects well with young people and adults is a rare combination, especially someone who is just beginning their new ministry calling. They also know that very few youth pastors stay for any length of time, but a wise and seasoned youth leader influences the entire church community. These results can make it much easier for a lead pastor as it influences positively other ministries that are under his or her leadership.

When young people are welcomed and integrated into the relational fabric of the wider church family, it usually becomes a contagious segment of the population that infuses energy, life and vitality into the entire church community. The key is that the youth leader needs to work well with the other ministry leaders, especially the senior pastor, and then to enfold the student population into the overall vision and mission of the church. If the youth leader can motivate students to serve in other ministries such as children's, seniors, worship and missions, the senior pastor and leadership team will be deeply grateful and supportive.

In many churches, the success of the youth pastor can be intimidating to other staff members, or even to the senior leadership, because their visibility and energy can impact deeply the entire church family. It is essential that the youth leader be on the same page as the overall leadership team of the church. Even with a successful youth ministry, if it is not in co-operation with the direction of the church membership the youth pastor can be seen as non-conformist and breed dissension among the other church staff. That would make it a no-win situation for the senior pastor. If the relationship between the senior pastor and the youth leadership is strong, youth ministry can often be the growth engine for the church and the spirit of unity makes it a special and a fulfilling place to minister.

Chapter 10

Lorna McIntosh from Scotland

My chapter is dedicated to Duncan, Ross and Fiona, my family and biggest supporters.

1. My background and how I got into youth ministry

I come initially from Glasgow and moved to Falkirk, a little town in Scotland, when I got married. For the last 12 years I have served as the youth pastor at St John's Church, Linlithgow, Scotland. Scotland is known all over the world for its tartan, kilts, mountains, lochs, castles, rain and whisky, but most importantly for the friendly people who live there. Edinburgh and Glasgow are the largest cities and Linlithgow, where I work, is located in between.

Looking back I now believe that God was calling me into youth ministry from a very early age, but I did not realise this until I was actually in my 30's. I became a Christian as a young girl and was baptised at the age of 17 when my faith became real and my relationship with Jesus became important to me. I left school around the same time and went to work in a local bank. I met Duncan and we got married when I was 21. We have two children, Ross and Fiona.

I love the fact that I married young and have been blessed with two lovely children. Yet for many years, whilst I do not at all regret the decision to marry and have children, my life carried on just happening without really giving God space to use me. It seemed *I* was in control of my life rather than God.

Beginnings

I started helping with youth work at a Brethren Church in Falkirk and very quickly found myself taking charge of that work while I was working full time for the bank and bringing up the children. I ran the youth club and taught the Bible to young people for many years before I felt God nudging me - in fact, giving me a real kick - to leave my job and concentrate on youth work full time. Even in my job I ended up working with teenagers when I was asked to teach youth classes on finance and budgeting. I didn't realise it then but God was training me for what was to come!

However, when I shared with the church my heart to work with young people they did not understand! My heart was broken by this as I loved the people in the church and the young people I was working with. I did not want to leave. I was already struggling with insecurities and doubt because I was 38 years of age, which in the UK is old for a youth pastor, and also a woman in a church that did not believe that women could have any position of leadership whatsoever.

I was wrestling with God about why he was leading me in this direction; I just did not seem to 'fit'. But my husband and my children kept supporting and encouraging me - they are still my greatest source of support and encouragement. I knew I needed to move from that church if I was to be true to my calling. I did so despite leaving behind many people, old and young, that I loved. I stepped out in faith with my family cheering me on.

Studies

I wanted to be the best youth worker I could and went to Bible College to study Youth Ministry. This was quite daunting for me as I am not very academic. I studied at International Christian College in Glasgow, Scotland, and completed a degree in Youth Ministry and Applied Theology in 2006. It was during my second year of studies that I moved from the church in Falkirk (that didn't understand my calling) to join the staff team at St John's who very much understood it and embraced my family too.

A town and not a house

Linlithgow is a small town around about 15 miles from where I live. It is also the town where my sister has lived for many years. When I drove into the town to visit my sister my heart would race as I passed the first house there. I told my husband Duncan that God was going to give me that house one day to make into a home for young people. Sometimes we get it wrong! God was actually calling me to work in that town. He was calling me to the town, not the house! So when the job in St John's became available I had confidence and applied. I have been here for 12 years and have loved every minute and every young person. When God gives you a heart for a job, and a calling for a place, it is very hard to leave.

2. Looking after your own soul

When I started working as a full time youth worker I was surprised at how difficult it was to keep yourself connected to God. You may think that working all day every day for the Creator, your Saviour and Lord will keep your relationship with him strong and safe. However, that is not the case. Very quickly your faith can turn into work, and your devotions turn into preparation for youth meetings. Before you realise it your relationship with the Lord can go downhill.

But over the years I have been blessed with good people getting alongside me to help and support and keep me on track. I would suggest you do the same, whoever you are! These people asked me the right questions and challenged me about my spiritual life in a way that was sometimes harsh but necessary.

Here are four practical things that I do:

- I make sure that I attend a good conference at least twice a year, where I can receive from God.
- Every month I meet with other youth workers. During this time we pray for each other and give each other space and time.
- For my personal devotions I use two different things: the Bible and a good Christian book. This gives me some diversity.
- When I am driving I don't listen to the radio but instead try to listen to God.

3. Singleness, Marriage and Children

I wouldn't be doing this job if it wasn't for my husband and children telling me that I was good at what I did. Duncan is my champion and he supports me fully in all my silly plans and ideas. There have been many times when I have been at work and a family crisis (my family) has happened; Duncan has never complained or questioned my loyalty. When his mother passed away I was running a youth camp for 60 young people. I couldn't just leave them and head home. Duncan understood that and has never complained.

Recently a group of young people told me that I was a 'mumsy' youth worker, i.e. like their mothers. I took this as a compliment. I am a mum to two lovely children, Ross and Fiona, and they have shaped me into who I am, so I am proud of that. As a mum I wanted to help my children be the best that they could possibly be and in my job I do the same with each young person that I work with. I want to release the full potential that God has placed within each one.

So, what have I learned from that is that you need to be yourself; and if you are married make sure your spouse also shares your sense of calling - that way they will understand why you work so hard!

4. Organising yourself and your ministry

I work to a rhythm within my ministry. I run three terms. I like to keep it simple:

- Summer to Christmas: Evangelism
- Christmas to Easter: Discipleship
- Easter to end of Summer: Mission

As you see, each term has a clear purpose. This helps ensure that the youth ministry overall is rounded. We do not want to concentrate too much time on just one or two areas of ministry for the whole year.

There is a key activity during each term. For example, the 'Alpha' Course in September, a discipleship weekend at Easter, and Holiday Club and overseas mission trip in the summer.

5. Keeping your evangelism edge sharp

It is important to keep your own focus on evangelism and mission sharp in order to keep the youth work proactive. In this way you are 'doing' together rather than just 'being' together. It is easy for you and for them to 'be' group together and enjoy creating community, but you can also hide behind this and think that young people are too young in the faith to do evangelism and mission. Remember, evangelism and mission is what we are all called to do: let's be fishers of men!

Groups of youth naturally enjoy spending time with people they are comfortable with. But unless you keep changing how that group looks, and challenge the group to expand, you will get into a situation where the group grows up together without evolving. They eventually grow out of the youth programs and leave, with no younger youth coming through. Your youth work should be such a good fit and exciting for your young people that they want to bring friends along; they will comfortably talk about what they are doing in church and that will naturally bring new people along. Keep encouraging the young people to be accepting and inclusive and show them how to do that.

I have three key points that I would like to share:

- Read quality publications monthly so you keep up to date with new initiatives in evangelism and mission
- Link with good national organisations that feed you with inspiring emails
- Model a 'doing' attitude amongst your team of leaders

The most important of these is the last. You have to model the 'doing' attitude. It is important to actually get out there and achieve something! I have spent time with many church youth workers who talk about taking young people on mission, talk about running a course for evangelism, and talk about running an event to highlight the social and economic issues of our day; but don't get out there and actually do it! If you say to your youth that mission is important, then you need to follow through and get on with it. Stop talking and go and do!

We have been taking teams of youth to Rwanda since 2008 but that takes a lot of preparation and planning and is not easy for everyone to do. There are smaller events that you can do which have a big impact on young people and help keep your youth ministry fresh and current. They can be fun events with a serious educational focus. Here are some of the smaller things we have done.

We made a 'slum village' in our local high street using wooden pallets. We had a 'Syrian' sleep over night where every hour the young people lose more and more of their belongings. To help them understand what it might be like to be a refugee we slept overnight in a transit van to understand more about 'people trafficking'. We held a 'secret church' event to highlight the persecuted church. Last year we ran a 'Socks and Chocs' project at Christmas where we wrapped a new pair of warm socks and a bar of Chocolate and went to our nearest city, Edinburgh, and handed the presents out to homeless people on the street. We offered to pray for the people and no-one refused the prayer or the gift of chocolate and socks. The youth loved it as they felt empowered; the cost was affordable and so everyone felt involved; the young people felt that they had made a small difference to some really needy people at a time of year when it is very difficult being homeless. We also made a film while doing this that was uploaded to YouTube and shared at our church nativity service.

6. Communicating with youth

Teaching young people is very different from teaching adults or children. There is a key to getting the teaching right. As children grow into young adults they start to form their opinions. I believe that as youth workers it is important for us to help them wrestle with what they think about what they read in the Bible. This enables them to get excited about their faith and grow in their faith rather than just listen to what we as youth workers think everything means. That may seem easy to do, but it is actually really hard not to push your own agenda onto the young people and share what your own theology is. They will remember things for longer and it will have more impact on their lives if they have reached the answer, opinion or truths by their own thinking, work and deductions. Saying that, however, doesn't mean that I don't prepare teaching and don't deliver teaching! I just prepare it in a way that allows them to discuss, debate and even question what I am teaching.

Here are three things I have learned:

- 'Issue-based' teaching allows you to cover things that your youth are struggling with, like bullying, sex, addictions, etc, but is more effective if done in small chunks rather than every week.
- 'Systematic' teaching covering the Bible allows them to wrestle with difficult passages that would often be left out and ignored, so they get a good chance to explore the Bible. This can be time consuming.
- 'Synchronise' your teaching with what the adults in the rest of the church are doing. This can be helpful as families can discuss over

the dinner table what has been taught at church. You need good communication with the person preaching the sermon so that the same points are covered!

There are no right or wrong ways to teach young people. I use a mixture of the above. Basically, the more you can get them to open up the Bible and ask the Holy Spirit to guide their thoughts as they read, and allow them to discuss with each other and older Christians, the better their faith will grow.

7. Pastoral care of young people

One of the key ways in which I provide pastoral care for young people is by praying for them. By praying for them I am led by the Spirit to discern whether they need a chat or a text or a message to be sent. Thinking about them one by one and praying for them one by one makes me realise when I last saw them, who is missing, who was looking sad or happy, or who was feeling a bit left out. It makes me focus my thoughts and helps me love and care for each one as an individual.

Small groups

On Sunday morning all the young people are together and we use this time to chat one to one with them or to a few together who need a bit of extra attention at that time. We have small groups running during the week. I really appreciate the opportunity to see the young people mid-week to catch up with how things are going with their week. Some of these groups are peer-led and are more like 'accountability' groups where they share problems and pray for each other. I love these groups since the best pastoral care is actually done by the young people *to* the young people without them actually knowing that they are doing it.

Deeper issues

When someone has a more complex issue to deal with we are able to offer one to one support. We meet the young person in a coffee shop or a fast food place. The conversation is private but is done in a public place and not in secret. This helps keep the young person and also the youth leader safe. This also keeps us in line with our church child protection policy. It is very sad that we now live in a culture that is suspicious and so damaging, but we need to be conscious of our surroundings at all times and not be naive.

If there are three things that I would like to pass on they would be:

- Remember that each young person is created as a unique individual, wonderfully and beautifully made - treat them that way and you will not fail
- Listen - and show that you are listening
- Don't Judge - Just Love

8. Working with schools

In Scotland it is very difficult to speak openly about Christianity. We have no platform for sharing the Gospel message in an open way within high school, but we can run a Bible group (called a 'Scripture Union' or 'SU' Group) within the school.

We are called to serve our local high school and that is what we try hard to do. We partner with the school and help in classes if and when it is appropriate to do so. For example, over the years I have helped with classes on interview skills for getting a job since that was the line of work I was in prior to being a youth worker. I have helped with difficult groups of young people who are not engaged in the general education process. I am also free to access the school and the teaching staff know me well. I am there at least once a week at the Scripture Union Group. This group meets as a lunch club and we chat over a Bible passage, play a game or two, and then pray. It is a simple structure and it is a safe space for people who need a little bit of 'sanctuary' during the school day. I would like to do more in school, and keep praying for opportunities to provide a 'prayer space' or some one-to-one counselling for pupils generally. I have faith that one day this will happen. I serve in whatever way I can.

One lesson I would pass on to from my work in schools would be to keep persevering and keep offering to help - don't give up and don't be disheartened, but just keep trying new ways to serve your school.

9. Leading a team and developing others

It is very important that you recognise that you will gravitate towards people who are like you, and that you will want to lead the youth ministry with your friends. However, that is not always the best idea as you will soon learn that you will be missing key essential qualities that you will not have covered. Let me explain what I mean.

I am a chatty, 'ideas' person who is very positive, with a 'can do' attitude. That is great; I like who I am and many of my friends are very similar to me. So if I am running an event or a youth weekend away I am great at coming up with creative ideas about what to do, the theme, the games and the fun elements. But I need others who will look into the detail as to how we will get these things done, e.g. what we will eat. I tend to find the detail boring but it is just as important as the creative ideas. With the right team combination the weekend away will be a success. So I need to ensure that my team is diverse and all areas of work are covered. The team need to be, and feel, very involved. We all have a role to play.

Over the years I have grown teams for a number of activities, like the discipleship weekend away I mentioned earlier. This team now consists of ex-youth (now graduates and students) and two wonderful cooks! I have a completely separate team for summer camps because I need more of a pastoral team with some key adults who can get alongside the youth, pray for them and be with them. I also need competent drivers and physically strong people who can look after a campsite, a marquee and cook for lots of young people in a field for a week. That takes a great team, and mine is the best!

So remember:

- Diversity is key
- Play to individual strengths
- Communicate well - keep meetings brief and concise
- Develop young people into leaders

It is important to train and equip your team and it pays to invest in them. My teams are invited each year to attend a youth work conference in the north of Scotland called Deep Impact which is for youth workers and volunteers. Going away for a fun weekend together bonds a team and shows that you value them and appreciate all that they do. It also inspires them, develops them, teaches them and refuels them. Find out what is near you that is like this or run your own weekend of training for your team.

10. Parents

I probably find this much easier than many youth workers because I am also a parent and am the same age as many parents of the young people.

A help or a threat

Many parents over the years have related well with me as they feel that they can chat with me as an equal about their son/daughter. However, I have also experienced the opposite as some parents can see me as a threat. When their son/daughter is growing a bond with you that parents don't initially appreciate or understand they can become jealous and resentful. You need to watch out for this and keep it in mind as you work closely with youth.

Communication

Good communication is essential in our line of work. It is important to let parents know when you are meeting, where and what events are happening, and if something is cancelled or changed let them know as far in advance as possible. Parents are busy people and do not take kindly to last minute changes of plans. Parent consent forms may seem like a painful grind to you, but to parents it says, "This person is working as a professional and is looking after our child's interests properly, and I now know the relevant details of what is going on".

Confidentiality

You do not need to disclose every conversation that you have with a child to their parent/s. For example, a parent may feel that they need a debrief after a one-to-one conversation that you had in some coffee shop with their son or daughter. But it will not be beneficial to that young person or to your relationship with them if you instantly share everything they said to their parent/s without their consent. What you do need to do is reassure the parent/s that everything is OK and let them know that you would share any necessary information that they need to know.

11. You and senior church leaders

I am very blessed in my church, St John's, as I am on the leadership team of the church as well. The Senior Pastor and other leaders love the youth work and the young people. In fact, they see them as key to all that happens in the church. I can share openly with the leaders the plans and the vision for the youth work. I know that the leadership will add value to this vision and support it fully. Our young people are very visible in church; they lead worship, pray openly, teach others, share testimony, serve on various church teams and are loved in the church by old and young alike.

However, I know this is not the case in many churches here. When mentoring other youth workers I have seen the struggles that they have with their church leaders. One of the most common is the lack of understanding and acceptance of what youth work actually is. Often the leadership still view the youth work as more of a babysitting service or something that 'keeps them in line', i.e. a passive type of ministry rather than one that empowers and inspires young people to become the men and women that God wants them to be. Budgets are often minimal, acceptance is normally lacking, the profile of the youth ministry is usually low, and opportunities for youth to be active in service are generally non-existent.

The best advice I have been given over the years about training and releasing youth into areas of service in the church is what I would call 'Tightropes and Safety Nets'. When putting youth into an area of service or ministry make sure that, as they step into something new, you put a safety net in place so that if it all goes wrong they will be able to bounce back and be able and willing to try again.

To work well with your church leader, meet regularly and share your heart, reflect honestly on how your work is going, and make sure you don't hide what is not working. Ask for help with improving your work. Above all else try not to be defensive about your work or you will find it hard to take wise criticism and use it to benefit your work.

Chapter 11
Mark Stoorvogel from The Netherlands

My chapter is dedicated to Marin, Ivan and Marko. My friendship with you brought me into youth ministry in the first place. Love you guys!

1. My background and how I got into youth ministry

My parents and my brothers always demonstrated by the way they live that when you really give yourself for something, nothing is impossible. From the age of seventeen I travelled each year from Holland to Chattanooga, Tennessee in the USA to work with a local church. I took part in volunteer work serving children and teenagers in the inner city. I participated in youth camps, organized trips and fun outings, and I visited families in their homes.

During my first trip I was warned never to go out on the streets alone, especially after 7pm; but as I kept coming back each year, I grew close to some of these families and they would actually host me as I stayed in their city for periods of time. More than once I found myself playing hide and seek in the streets, in the middle of the night, with these kids who had no curfews or bedtimes. God gave me a deep love for these people, and I gladly did anything for them. I shared my heart, and even my life.

After a few years I had made up my mind: I was going to devote my life to the families of the inner city in Chattanooga. However, what I had envisioned did not happen, no matter how I tried. After two and a half years of trying to get a visa I had to face the fact that my application still hadn't come through, and it probably never would. I gave up my dream and I entered into a very dull season of my life. I did not understand why God did not open the doors for me to go to the USA. I told myself that this was part of growing up, to give up your dreams and just go live life the way everybody else does.

But then, during a conference in Holland, Bill Wilson, the leader of a very successful children's church in New York City, was speaking. The core message of his sermon was: 'One man can make a difference'. As I

listened, I realized I had once believed that, but I had lost that convic-
tion. As the altar call came, I ran forward and asked Jesus to renew my
faith and give me a new dream to live for. God then started to speak to
me about just that. I saw a presentation concerning the massive number
of young people leaving the church and it struck me. Some teenagers at
the conference started coming to me for help as they were struggling
with various matters. God made me aware of the fact that I could be
doing the same things here as in America. I did not need a new dream.
His plan for my life had not changed, but it was never bound to a specific
location!

A few months after this conference, a job offer came my way. The
church I was a part of was growing and the leaders recognized the importance of a well-functioning youth ministry. Therefore they needed a
youth pastor. I was asked to apply for the position, and I did not have to
think about it for very long, for God had already called me! Since 2007, I
have been working full-time at the Independent Baptist Church in Gron-
ingen, an evangelical church in the North of Holland. Within 25 years,
this church has grown from 6 people to over 1500! One third of this community consists of 12-30 year olds. This goes to show that in a country
where church attendance - especially among youth - is not guaranteed
any more, God is in fact building churches where people of all ages come,
not because they feel obliged, but because they have a deep personal con-
viction that draws them. I feel driven to give myself fully to the church of
Jesus Christ in Holland, because one man can make a difference!

2. Looking after your own soul

I almost cracked under the pressure. I love working long hours for
the church. I also love having lots of different tasks and responsibilities.
I love all the different kinds of people that I meet. The thing I could not
handle though, were the expectations. Being raised as the son of a minis-
ter/pastor, I already knew that people do not always have a very realistic
view of full time ministry workers, or their family lives. But still, there
was that sense of having to be a little more spiritual, a little more holy, a
little more devoted than others.

As the church was growing rapidly, and I had accepted a full time
position in it, the unrealistic expectations did start to affect me. Many
teams were incomplete, and all of them needed me to jump in and fill the

holes. Many teenagers needed my personal attention. Then there were the many others that hoped I would help with their personal issues. And no matter how hard I worked, it never felt like I was done. I could not meet everybody's needs, but that was not what bothered me the most. I especially struggled with the fact that I wasn't as spiritual as people wanted me to be. I was haunted by painful memories from my youth; I was fighting all sorts of worldly temptations and I was angry with God because I felt He had given me more than I could handle.

I started to resent people with their sky high expectations of me, because I knew I was falling short. So I cried out to God: "I know You want me in this position, but I don't want to do it anymore!!". Jesus started to lovingly teach me. I sense He said to me: "Mark, I knew what I was getting into when I called you. I believe in you. Don't give up. Live life based on My victory". Slowly it started to dawn on me that youth ministry, or the church, isn't about people and what they expect and want and need. It is about Jesus. And the things that He has called me to are not too heavy, because He provides everything that is needed. I have one assignment, one calling and one ministry, and that is to love the Lord my God with all that is within me.

It is important for me to regularly have some distance from the church. I plan little get away moments in my schedule every week, but on top of that, I undertake some sort of trip abroad every year to detach myself from the demands back home. My ideal 'getaways' are those trips where I don't know where I will sleep the next day. Freedom! Just a break from everything. But although I have 'church-less' days, I never wish to go a day without Jesus. Time and time again I need to feed on the Living Word of Jesus to hold fast to the truths that He reveals in it. To remind myself of this, I put a quote by Mike Bickle on the wall in my office that says: "I have to remind myself that I am not called to be a spiritual politician that needs to be at every church activity. I am called to be a man filled with holy passion and affection for Jesus. That is what I want to minister to people". I want to walk out that calling in my lifetime.

3. Singleness, marriage and children

There is an considerable increase in the number of single people living in Holland, especially in larger cities. One of the main causes of this phenomenon is modern individualism. This culture in which we live heavily influences our desire and convictions. One of the consequences is wanting to find the perfect partner that fits those desires and convictions.

I myself have also been influenced by this culture that surrounds me every day. I am 34 years old and unmarried. I have been single for most of my years in full time youth work. There have been moments where I have felt lonely and like no one really knew me. I longed for a partner in my life. A woman by my side could strengthen me and my ministry in so many ways. Also, I believe that God made mankind to be relational, and that the biblical picture of marriage gives us a vision for the relationship Christ wants to have with us, His bride, the Church. Even though I was open to meeting women and finding someone who would add something unique to my life, that did not happen. I decided that, as long as I did not find a woman who would really complement me, I would remain alone.

There are advantages to being single: it gave me plenty of opportunity to see the world, and to invest my time in ministry and personal contact with teenagers. Through all of this I have learned that Jesus is the ultimate fulfilment for every need that I have and that by receiving Him, I have received everything.

Being single is not always easy, but it does give opportunities for ministry and life in God you might not otherwise have entered into. Waiting for the right person might sound passive. Brian Houston (Hillsong, Sydney) once said: "Are you waiting for the perfect woman to walk into your life? Nothing wrong with that. But do make sure that you can be the perfect man for her when she meets you, otherwise she may not even notice you and keep walking". I wanted to be ready to be that man, a man who loves his wife the way Jesus loves the Church. I realise this is a lofty goal and that it will take a lifetime to even come close to that picture, but Jesus has worked in me powerfully during the past few years, and I believe I will make a much better husband now than I would have 10 years ago. But whether single or married, I will always pursue my Lord Jesus and His Kingdom!

4. Organising yourself and your ministry

Something had to change! The numbers showed that we had about twenty 12 to 15 year olds, but only three or four of them would actually show up at the youth group meetings we organized. And that was only because their parents made them go! The youth leaders would come up with a theme for the evening as they went, and looked up some portions of scripture to back that up. They meant well, but the kids would just sort of 'make it through' an evening and wait for the chips and sodas to be served. I told those leaders: this has to change!

It's easy to be critical, but are you willing to BE the change you want to see? When I was nineteen, a group of us started doing youth work at our church. We were not very organized, but we did have a lot of vision. Organization follows vision, not the other way around. Our youth work began to develop, slowly but steadily. Since then, we started working through so called 'task forces'. The youth work consists of eight different task forces, each having their own area of focus. There are task forces for small groups, services and evangelism, etc. They are led by volunteers, which I used to direct by myself, but I now share that responsibility with a team called a 'base group'. The base group cares for all the task force leaders and ensures healthy development of all task forces, based on four pillars: Intimacy with God; Personal Development; Looking out for one another; and World Focus. The members of the base groups and the task forces are the ones within the organization that I devote my time and attention to.

The youth work in our church started out small, but it has become bigger and bigger. This demonstrates a principle that I believe in: to think big, and start small. I see churches struggling to make their youth work successful, but nothing develops because there is no vision or dream behind what's being done. Also, some ministries feel disappointed when big plans and huge events are implemented but results turn out to be very limited. It's not big events and cool activities that build healthy youth work, it's relationships. And building relationships takes time. It's good to dream about many young people finding their way to God and the church, but start with the ones God has already given you. Build on that, reach for more and you will find that nothing is impossible for the one who believes!

5. Keeping your evangelism edge sharp

Every Wednesday night, from October through March, dozens of youngsters from the neighborhood flood our church. They come to play sports, to hang out and to meet friends. The church turns into a community center with two ping pong tables, a foosball table and a hockey field.

Behind the church we play soccer in a large cage, and the coffee house is open for hanging out and enjoying coffee and a chat. In our opinion, evangelism equals relationship and sport is a powerful tool through which to build those relationships.

A few years ago, a group of young people took a soccer ball and some flyers to a nearby playing field in the hope of meeting some young people from the area. Three guys came, and that number stayed the same for months. But the group said: "If God gives us these three boys, then we will give our all for them". That loyalty began to produce more fruit over time. Nowadays, more than fifty kids come to 'FaceOff', which is what this sports ministry was named. Some youth show up just every now and then, but a steady number come in every week. They come from different backgrounds and cultures. Many of them are Muslim, some have a grandparent who is a Christian, and some never contemplated the existence of a God. During the summer we meet them outside.

During winter, when it is too cold and dark to be outside, we invite them to the church building. During the breaks, when everyone catches their breath from playing sports, we tell them Bible stories and testimonies of our lives with Jesus. Some kids have decided to accept Jesus into their lives, and some even made the choice to be baptized and join the church.

In the past few years I have learned that a building makes all the difference in how young people view the church. We tend to say that WE are the church, but for neighborhood youth we are just a part of the overall picture. Many of them were a little tense about entering the building, as if setting foot in the church would immediately make them Christians. But when they did come in, they were often surprised: "It doesn't look like a church at all!". They seemed to draw the conclusion that when the building turned out to be nothing like they expected, maybe the church itself was also different from what they thought. This lowered the threshold for them to come in on a Sunday and attend a service.

It is not just the neighborhood kids that benefit from the FaceOff ministry. One of the goals is that young people from the church take part and grow in discipleship. The team comes together every Wednesday to start with a meal, teaching, worship and prayer. First the team members receive, and then they go and share. Some of them are very young, they make friends with the kids that visit. Others are more mature, they keep order and coach the others in their activities. All in all, relationship happens! So FaceOff is here to stay, in our church and in our neighborhood!

6. Communicating with youth

In The Netherlands, most lesson material available in the Dutch language is focussed on life skills. So youth work here can sometimes look like social skills training. We teach our teenagers to live in a way that is expected from Christians. But is this what we, as a church, are intended to be like? One of the biggest hazards I see in youth work, is the danger of 'second generation Christianity'. I have seen it happen all around me in The Netherlands: youngsters who go to church with their parents or because it is what you are supposed to do. But the reality shows that God does not have any grandchildren. God is our Father, not our grandfather. Every generation has to make a well-considered choice for Jesus Christ, the only way to the Father.

By having life skills as their starting point, the Christian life soon becomes too stringent; a set of rules. But when young people get to know the person of Jesus they are renewed from the inside out and this results in a life dedicated to Jesus through the Holy Spirit. In our youth ministry this has given us a clear focus on getting to know Jesus Christ and knowing what is in His heart for us. I have been asked several times what the key is to our flourishing youth work. The only response that I can give is that it is all about Jesus!

In the culture of the Netherlands there is a strong emphasis on a person's own experience. It is important to youngsters not only to hear the Word, but to also experience it in their lives. Initially, this happens through the work of the Holy Spirit in youngsters. We often give young people the opportunity to be prayed for after hearing the Word so the Holy Spirit has room to speak Truth in their lives. Experience also means doing. When your youth ministry becomes bigger, there is the danger of consumerism. Where you once did everything together as a youth group, now everything is being organised for you. Even though different programmes become better and better, this does not automatically mean your youngsters get better as well.

We want to challenge our youth to implement and develop their gifts and talents in worship, hospitality, evangelism, mission work, creative expression and preaching. Every gift and talent that the church is built on can also be found in young people. It is for us, youth pastors, to recognize potential in youngsters and let them use it. Obviously, this takes much time and effort, but I am convinced that this is exactly where our time and energy should go. The Word of God is alive! It is our valuable task to communicate it in a way that will empower young people to live out everything that God has in store for them!

7. Pastoral care of young people

Before starting my work at the church as the youth pastor I used to work at an institute for children and teenagers with psychiatric problems. In this institute I heard about the most bizarre and harrowing situations and I gained experience in dealing with a wide range of problems. By the time I started working for the church there was very little that unsettled or horrified me.

In my opinion, it is important that youth pastors acquire knowledge and insight about regularly occurring problems among youngsters, e.g. eating disorders, behavioural problems and self-harming. Just like the world, the church is filled with people who are damaged and hurt; this includes young people. Many churches are unaware of these problems. But the fact that you are not always aware of such problems does not mean that they are not present! Young people often have a tendency to make light of their problems and not ask for help until they seem to be drowning in their misery. As a youth worker, you may ask yourself, "Do we really see inside our young people?" or "Do we know what is going on in their lives?". We frequently invite our youngsters to come to us with their sorrows, their sin and their struggles. By having open, loving and merciful relationships with youth leaders and the continual offer to pray after church services, teenagers feel free to answer this invitation. Care should be available to everyone at all times.

A teenager's problems can be overwhelming. In my early years I thought it was important that every young person should be able to receive help and support from the church. From my background in social work I felt comfortable speaking with parents and teenagers when they no longer understood each other. I supported them when they were mourning the loss of a loved one. I counselled young people who were placed into care because they could no longer live at home. This took much of my time and as more young people came to the youth ministry I started realizing that I was setting unrealistic goals for myself. As a youth pastor, it is impossible to do everything. It is the same for social workers who have a limited amount of cases in their care. Many things are expected from a youth worker and it is impossible to jump into every difficult situation.

In helping young people in problematic situations, we as a church also need a professional support system. The welfare system in our country has many resources to help young people in specific situations. But as a church we have something that social welfare cannot offer: Jesus! He says: "Come to me, all you who are weary and burdened, and I will give you rest" (Matthew 11:28). Even in the most difficult of times we can invite youngsters to come to Jesus. We do not have to come up with all the answers, but Jesus is able to pull these young people out of every situation. Jesus has amazed me so many times by what He can do in young people's lives. Jesus cares!

8. Working with schools

In The Netherlands it is uncommon for churches to get entry into schools. There are certain traditional protestant schools that only admit pupils with a church background. In these, teachers may only teach when they belong to one of a small number of traditional churches. An evangelical high school can be found in the middle of our country, in an area where many Christians live.

A large number of teenagers in our Evangelical church go to a traditional protestant school. These schools have a good reputation, give space to the Christian faith, offer good education and take care of their pupils. Even so, the behaviour of the teenagers is not very different to those in other schools. In these schools there are also people who swear, have sex with each other and take drugs. I find that pupils in these schools can have more difficulty deciding where they stand in their faith than other Christian teenagers who go to other types of schools. Sometimes it is easier to make radical choices in a school where you are one of a few Christians than in a classroom where everyone says they believe in God without it being evident in their behaviour. When being asked for my advice, I often recommend that parents send teenagers to a regular school. As a youth pastor I may not have much access to schools, but as churches we present Jesus through our teenagers.

It is not always easy for our teenagers to stand tall as a Christian in schools, and I see this as an important task for the church. As a church, it is our duty to empower our youngsters to go into the world. It is of great importance that our teenagers see and believe that they can make a difference in the place where they spend most of their time. The segregation between church and school, originating during the last few decades in Holland, has also had some positive outcomes. It may not be customary for the church to be involved in schools but we observe that schools are starting to seek out the church more easily. A growing number of teenagers grow up outside the church, but curiosity is still there. At the moment, several schools rent our church building for their annual Christmas celebrations. This often leads people to come and visit our Sunday services. Furthermore, a group of pupils from a public school come to our church for an excursion every year to get a broader cultural perspective of our society. Last of all, we also get positive responses from schools on our involvement in the neighborhood, something their pupils talk about enthusiastically. These are small examples of a new open-heartedness towards the church. While society keeps changing, we as a church continuously seek for new ways to make a difference in it.

9. Parents

In youth ministry, never underestimate the influence of parents. Research shows that three out of four young people see their parents as the most important people in their lives. Even if we say we value parents it is often not reflected as much in our ministries in a practical sense.

I believe fathers are the most important people in the formation of the self-image of teenagers. It is wonderful to help in this. Not long ago we held our first parent-teenager afternoon for a small group of people. Most teenagers showed little interest and admitted that they had come after their parents had persuaded them to come. Looking back, they all had a wonderful day. Nonetheless, in my opinion the relationship between youth work and parents is not limited to organizing activities with parents. There are other ways to keep them involved in youth ministry. Parents can get involved through annual meetings where they get information about spiritual goals and activities for the months ahead, or by inviting them to join in at the end of a youth weekend to tell them what happened, or by speaking with them when they come to collect their children from youth group. Naturally, parents like to know what their children are experiencing. Most teenagers do not necessarily speak with their parents about these things! As youth workers we can help with this in an appropriate way.

Our church is also indirectly involved with a movement especially for men called *The 4th Musketeer*. The movement brings men closer to the heart of God, their family, church and righteousness through challenging activities and events. Out of my heart for teenagers, I co-initiated 'Father-Teenager' weekends a few years ago. Over long weekends, fathers spend time with their teenage sons or daughters in the hilly countryside of the Belgian mountain range called The Ardennes. Apart from physical activities like mountain biking, hiking, climbing, abseiling and sleeping on a campsite, fathers and teenagers receive teaching and assignments concerning the relationship they have with their heavenly Father and each other. It is very impressive to see fathers and sons bond together, and fathers and daughters grow in their love for each other during these weekends.

10. Leading a team and developing others

When I was first appointed as the youth pastor I was able to lead on my own and be involved in each part of our youth ministry. But with growth in mind, I did not want to limit the development of our youth work by always having to do everything and be involved in everything, otherwise the youth ministry could never grow bigger than I could handle by myself.

Bill George, Professor of Management Practice at Harvard Business School, wrote: "Leadership is empowering others to step up and lead". When I read this a couple of years ago I could only agree with him. Church leadership is often focused on organising and managing processes and activities, but genuine leadership has the development of others in mind. When others go for the vision wholeheartedly like you do, and believe in the same processes and activities, people will go for it with the same dedication and diligence as you do. This development in leadership requires the following four phases:

Directing

New volunteers are often uninformed about the vision of your ministry and can be doubtful about their own abilities. Young volunteers, who are still growing, often have to discover and practice leadership. Therefore, in this first phase the overall leader, in this case the youth pastor, is expected to give guidance. This means always explaining why we do things and giving clear instructions about how we do them. By doing so you create a safe environment where volunteers find security in what is asked of them.

Coaching

As soon as volunteers start to carry out their task, coaching becomes very important. Volunteers will need to know how you, as the overall leader, will judge how he or she performs in their role. In coaching them it is important to emphasise what is going well and to encourage them in what they are doing. Even though the volunteer is not completely accustomed to the vision or the way you do things he or she has become a part of it.

Supporting

At a certain point the volunteer will be able to take on more responsibilities without you having to tell them what to do. They now have the same passion and vision as you do and they know what needs to be done. But because the volunteer has been depending on your leadership, it is necessary for their confidence to grow in this phase. Consequently, your guidance will stop at this point, even though you will keep encouraging and supporting them when needed.

Delegating

Eventually the phase will begin where the volunteer is able to 'stand on their own two feet'. He or she does not need you anymore but can independently give their own contribution to the ministry. This is the time for you as a leader to step back and allow the volunteer to do their task and to delegate without you controlling them. The volunteer is empowered and can stand up and lead others as well.

11. You and senior church leaders

In my relationship towards my senior pastor I find the principle from Hebrews 13:17 very important. It says, "Have confidence in your leaders and submit to their authority, because they keep watch over you as those who must give an account. Do this so that their work will be a joy, not a burden, for that would be of no benefit to you". In this verse I am asked to help my leader – in this case my senior pastor – to fulfil his task with joy. To me, this means that I will do my very best to support him in his tasks, embrace his vision (sometimes after a heated discussion!) and always speak in a positive manner to him and about him.

My father was the senior pastor of my church for a long time, so I have seen up close how much of his time, effort, dedication and most of all his heart he put into the church. I have also seen how much negative criticism a senior pastor has to deal with. Ministry asks a lot of a senior pastor, and for this reason I think it is important that efforts are made to serve him in a way that brings him joy in his ministry. Thankfully, I have also seen how many people have been thankful for what my father meant in their relationship with God, even since he went to be with the Lord!

When I began in youth ministry my father was still serving as the senior pastor. This subsequently resulted in a double role for both of us. We were father and son as well as senior pastor and youth pastor. Because of this double role my father decided at my appointment that I would not work directly under his leadership, but that there would be someone in between. I still think this was a very wise decision. Nonetheless, a disadvantage was that the leadership of the youth ministry became detached from the overall leadership. The elders of the church often complained that it was not clear to them what the youth work involved and that they saw the youth ministry as an isolated part of the church.

A few years ago my father gave way to a new senior pastor, who is known to be a good team player. In a growing church he found it important that the leadership of the children's and youth ministries of the church would be fully integrated into the leadership team of the entire church. I see many youth pastors and youth workers in churches who struggle with their position in relation to the leadership of their church. I have come to the conclusion that youth ministry should not be considered as something that we have to do as a church, but that young people, together with children and adults, are all an integral part of the church and should be considered as such. Your senior pastor should find youth ministry just as important as you do!

I do realize that I am privileged to be in this position and that it is easier for me to serve and honour my leader compared to some other youth pastors. However, I believe that this biblical principle of leadership has a powerful impact, even for those who struggle with the relationship with their senior pastor. Make sure your leaders can fulfil their task with joy. Eventually, this will also benefit you.

SOME ADVICE WHEN LOOKING AT A YOUTH MINISTRY ROLE

Nathan from Nigeria

My first piece of advice is that you must understand that as a youth pastor you do not replace parents, who are a child's primary spiritual influence. Often as youth ministers we fall into the temptation of trying to impress the people interviewing us by telling them everything we can do with young people. But it is not all about us.

Secondly, be yourself. Do not try to create the impression that you are an expert just because you want to get the job. It is better to be honest than to give the wrong impression - let them know you are also growing.

Third, be sure you are clear about what you believe on key doctrines and on youth ministry so that you know how to respond to questions. If you get the job, your answers will only have enhanced your standing with the church leadership and make communication easier. You and they will be clear about what each believes.

Fourth, I would encourage you to learn something about the church you are applying to, e.g. the population, the leadership dynamics, the location, the key role players in the church. You can do that through a prior visit or getting information from the internet or through friends who attend the church.

Lastly, have any relevant documentation you need ready on the day of the interview.

Ron from Australia

Having moved to a new youth ministry role on three occasions, I know both the excitement as well as some of the fears associated with such a huge change. Assuming there is some match between you and the church/role, I would encourage serious consideration of the following five things:

1. What will be the impact on your family?

You may have your dream ministry opportunity. But will it be worth it if it does damage to your family? Your family is your primary ministry responsibility. Deuteronomy 6 and Ephesians 5-6 both encourage all Christians to carefully consider how they pass on faith in the family context. Paul takes this further when he instructs Timothy (1 Timothy 3) regarding overseers. Managing family is a significant requirement for church leadership. While we are not masters of the salvation of our children, we can be considerate and thoughtful about what is in their best interests.

As a Youth Minister, you are conscious of the value of friendships in lives, especially in young lives. Consider how a ministry move will impact *your* family and *their* social environment. When you move understand that due to your role you will develop relationships in a new community much quicker than them. Be considerate and thoughtful to the needs of your family. Consider also the perceived impact on their Christian journey.

2. Is there interpersonal chemistry with those you will be working with?

Spend some time with the people you will be working with. Try and find opportunities to connect with them in natural environments. Is there a natural chemistry that exists? You cannot avoid all potential relational problems, but having an awareness of some of them beforehand is helpful. This is so important that it could change your decision about taking up a role.

3. Will you have space to grow and develop?

Your growth in ministry will be beneficial to you, the church where you serve and the Kingdom of God. I am not suggesting that you need to move to a role that is 'bigger and better'. Growth could happen by changing context or by having different opportunities. If you aren't growing, you will become stale. When you are stale you will be bored. When you are bored you will either leave, or stay but just go through the motions of ministry. Neither will assist the longevity that is so valuable to youth ministry. Find somewhere to grow.

4. Understand the culture

Consider the culture of the area and church you will be ministering in. What are the core values? What are the struggles? What will you bring into that community? What barriers may exist to you loving that community? The youth ministry role is not (or should not) be carried out in a cultural vacuum. Ensure you know and understand the culture you are entering. Don't assume it's the same as yours, even if it's just across town!

5. The history and future of the church - where have they been, where are they going?

Discover the significant things that have taken place in the last 10 years of the church's life. The highs and the lows are important. What are they passionate about? What do they argue about? Similarly, discover where they are headed and the plans they have to get there. Is there alignment? Ministries that end badly after a short period are devastating for a pastor and their family, for the local church and for the Kingdom. Do the hard work beforehand to give all involved the best possible outcome.

Fraser from Scotland

I served in three churches in three countries and met many youth pastors from all types of churches along the way. From mine and their experience here are a few things you may want to think about:

1. Leave your current position/job well

Whatever it is, if you don't leave well I *guarantee* it will catch up with you somehow. It is the same for anyone in any job, but especially those in a pastoral role. Your character and reputation are central. How do you want to be remembered?

2. Doctrine and values

This often matters less to younger youth pastors for the simple reason that they have less life and ministry experience, less theological learning and practice, and so ask fewer questions! In some senses this makes it simpler. As you study the Bible and get older you clarify what you believe and these things matter even more deeply to you and you become less willing to compromise on your 'essentials'. So if you are just starting out write down a few key things you value and that you understand about church, and about youth ministry. It's a bit like dating or courtship. Do you like the people, the leaders? Does the doctrine of the church fit with what you believe? Write it down before the Lord and keep it to yourself and your spouse (if you have one). I did this before I interviewed for two out of my three roles and it helped significantly in helping sense whether God was calling me to a specific place and people, not just 'trying to get a job'.

3. Job description and terms and conditions

Read these carefully and clarify any points at the interview or via email (so it's in writing). People who write job descriptions can write one thing but mean another; the youth pastor being interviewed can read one thing but understand it to mean something else! I have seen youth pastors leave positions in less than a year because some things were not made clear or were not properly agreed upon - and then things start to fall apart after a few months. Make sure the job fits who you are or aspire to be. There should be proper supervision and regular evaluation of your role built into the job. You will not get rich in youth ministry, but you should be provided for sufficiently so your family is not 'killed on the altar of ministry' because of poor pay and/or unrealistic expectations. I ruled out several youth ministry roles right away when I saw the advert because of the level of pay and unrealistic expectations. If everything else seems to fit then get outside advice before you agree to come, and don't be scared of having an informal discussion with the lead pastor about expectations and pay. If it is a volunteer role it will not need to be nearly as exhaustive, but it needs to be clear to everyone what is expected of you, and what is expected of your supervisor.

4. Family needs

Make sure your spouse is completely with you. Two oxen in the yoke together cannot plough in different directions. If you have kids then seek to 'move when they move', i.e. when they are making a major transition in their education. If you are moving countries, then allow ample time for this; we took two years to think about, decide and then make the move abroad.

5. The lead/senior pastor

It is important you meet with them before you move into a new role. If you get on with them, great. If it is clear that you don't, then do not go there. Chemistry is part of a calling, just as character and competency are. If the lead pastor is not willing to meet with you personally then I would not go to that church because it shows they do not really value youth ministry, a key area in the life of the church they help lead.

6. The interview

These can vary widely. For one position I was one of three candidates interviewed over the same weekend. In another I stayed with one of the pastors (and his family with four children, three of them teenagers) for several days. There should be some sort of interview, even if the leadership knows you well. Prepare your answers to any questions you may have been given in advance. Be yourself at interview and when you meet the young people (teenagers will see straight through any pretence anyway). If there is not time to get answers to all your questions then follow up by email (so you get replies in written form).

IF YOU ARE THINKING OF LEAVING FRONT LINE MINISTRY

Very few youth pastors stay in vocational church youth ministry for life. Many move on from youth ministry in their 30's, some in their 40's, and a very small percentage in their 50's and beyond. Only those of us who have moved on from hands-on local church youth ministry have written for this last section.

Ron from Australia

The fact that you are reading this section shows you are at least ready to entertain the idea that there may be ministry beyond youth ministry. In my early years of ministry I was stubbornly convinced that I would be involved in hands-on youth ministry until the end of my working life. In fact, I resented people suggesting otherwise. Youth ministry made my blood pump; stability was a critical aspect of effectiveness, and I wasn't going to desert the cause!

Things have changed. My heart still beats for youth ministry, but I now serve in a church where I am no longer the youth pastor. It hasn't always been a smooth or easy transition, but it has been a good one. Here are four things I'd encourage you to consider as you contemplate moving on from youth ministry.

Be Honest

Front line youth ministry involves energy and creativity. There comes a point where the levels of energy and creativity required for hands on youth ministry are no longer sufficient to do that job. It's not a lack of will, it's a recognition that I am no longer as helpful as I once was and that handing over the ministry to someone else is critical. Recognising it's time to move on comes with its own anxieties. What will I do next? What will happen to the youth ministry I have invested in? While these questions come with valid concerns, there is also an exciting opportunity to grow in faith and entrust both yourself and the ministry into the hands of God.

Be helpful

Sometimes people with great motives get in the way. Don't be like that. Talk to those around you about the most helpful way for you to move on. Be aware that people with relational connections to you may not always be the most objective. Remember you want to serve the church, and the youth ministry. It may be best for their sake to have a clean break. I have remained in the same church and have broader responsibilities now. The first three years were about providing some oversight to the youth ministry as it transitioned. I imagine that within another few years I will have little to do with any of the decisions regarding youth ministry in our church.

Be a resource

If you have had over ten years in youth ministry you probably have a lot of wisdom to offer the Church. Consider how you can resource youth ministry in different ways. Be an advocate amongst parents and church leaders. Be an encourager to the youth leadership team. Perhaps there are opportunities to mentor and develop younger youth ministers or youth leaders. Use all you have learned and experienced to help others involved in hands-on youth ministry. For me, this is a great outlet for the beats of my heart that will always be for youth ministry.

Don't look back

I was thinking about the story of Lot and his wife (Genesis 19). The good news is that if you look back, you're not going to turn into a pillar of salt! But don't look back anyway. As you move on to other ministries, focus again on ministering in the present. Take all that you have learned with you. Approach your new challenges with eyes that look forward, and with energy for the places God has put you and will put you.

Fraser from Scotland

My hands-on youth ministry role ended when I was 46, a couple of years ago. But as is often the case with most older youth pastors, my role in the church had been expanding beyond youth ministry for some time.

I served for many years as an elder/pastor as part of the senior leadership team; not only was I leading the youth team but I was overseeing crèche to college ministries and giving particular attention to training and discipleship across the church. It was inevitable that I would leave hands-on youth ministry entirely; the question was when. In my context I knew it would probably mean moving on from that particular church. Two things were important to me. One was leaving well, i.e. on good terms with people. The other was making sure the various ministries I was leading, including youth ministry, were in as good a shape as possible when I left. This meant giving even more time to training others.

Like a plant being moved

Some time before I left youth ministry I began asking deep questions about the past twenty years of work and ministry, and thinking about the next twenty years. I felt very unsettled; but, all things considered, it just did not make sense to leave my youth ministry role at that time. Some people around that age experience an inner 'mid-life' crisis and make reckless decisions; others can get depressed. One morning I went for a walk and cried out to the Lord to speak to me. He graciously spoke, calmed my soul and made it very clear that He was teaching me things that I would later appreciate. I was to remain where I was. It was an important moment.

When I shared this story with a close friend, Brad, he shared a helpful illustration. He said that when you move a plant you don't just rip it up otherwise you can destroy the plant. You first gently disturb the soil around the roots before carefully moving the entire plant. So, being a perfect gardener, God was gently disturbing the soil around me (e.g. circumstances, prophetic words), and within me (my desires). A few years later my wife and I were talking and both had a simple but clear sense that my time at the church was coming to an end. So a few months later I was able to tell the other leaders that I intended to resign my role. This was nine months before I actually left, safe in the knowledge that it was God's will and not a rash decision.

Moving on gives room for others

Resigning well in advance gave the other leaders and the church ample time to consider how best to replace me and the various functions I was fulfilling. Two younger leaders I had spent time investing in ended up taking over much of what I had been doing. God kept me where I was for longer because I still had things to pass on. Another passion was also slowly brewing in me: writing. It is one reason I have taken time out of vocational ministry and taken a regular job so I can write in the evenings. This book is one result. The other book *Leadership Development with the One who Beat Goliath* is aimed at leaders in the first half of their life and leadership. Go to my website www.firsthalfleadership.com for more details.

A second curve

I have also found the *Sigmoid curve* helpful in terms of thinking about making major life and work transitions.

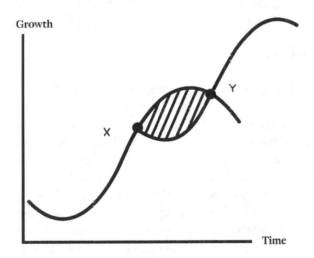

Author Charles Handy uses it in his book *The Age of Paradox* and applies it to individuals as well as organisations. Basically, he argues that the skills that get us a job and develop in it are often *not* the ones that keep us in it. So one solution is to start a 'second curve' in our career (point X) before the first one starts to decline some time later (point Y). That dip at the start of both curves on the graph is where we are slowly getting to grips with a new role, skill or situation. The shaded area is a period of uncertainty as you slowly transition between the two.

If you are in part or full time youth ministry your role *will* slowly change over the years. It is part of developing, and as in any other voca-tion, it is inevitable. If you are doing the same things in the same way you did them five years ago then you are probably stagnating - point Y. It's really about anticipating and developing the change ahead before things begin to decline. Ask yourself where you are at on the first curve? What are you most successful at? What do you enjoy doing most? What skills are transferable? It might be obvious, it might not be. A good supervi-sor or team leader should anticipate and make room for your growth, encouraging you to grow in other areas of ministry and talking with you about your leadership development. Talk with them, fellow youth work-ers you trust and, if married, your spouse. Reflect. Look around you. It may give you a clue as to what, if any, changes or moves might look like. Look to the Lord for what a second curve might involve, e.g. associate pastor, teacher, lead pastor or something totally different? God knows what He is doing. He loves you, the worker, not just the work.

Matt from Wales

The advantages of an experienced youth minister

If you are in church youth ministry and you are any good you will inevitably get drawn into other areas of church life. There are always other things to do that are positive and good, but it is vital to prioritise things and give yourself to the most important. I say all this because a great youth leader will be able to transfer their skills to all areas of church life. They can lead well in anything because they have leadership, people skills, and integrity. A mature youth minister often ends up pro-viding leadership for young adults and children as well as teenagers. It is therefore vital that the volunteer team are equipped and empowered to do the youth ministry as well as they possibly can. If the young people are familiar with the other people having significant roles then it won't be a major shock to them when you are not there doing all the hosting, leading and teaching.

Set things up to succeed

Try to set up things up so that whoever replaces you can soar. A youth minister is not excellent if things come crashing down in their absence;

they are excellent because, when they leave, it all keeps going because the culture, values and team are all in place. So do what you need to do, and fight any battles you need to in order to establish a strong culture that values youth ministry.

Plan regular reviews

Discerning the best time to move on is not the easiest of things to do, but if you can keep talking with the right people you won't become the 'elephant in the room' that others think needs to move on! It is worth having milestones, e.g. once a year, when you and your youth ministry are reviewed. If your senior leaders are not doing this then make sure it happens, even if you need to give them the questions to ask you.

Anne from The Philippines

Alliance Graduate School pioneered a Master of Arts degree in Youth Ministry in 1997, the first in Asia, and almost two decades later, is still the only Seminary offering such a major. The first visiting Youth Ministry professor to our seminary was 60-year-old 'veteran' Dan Jessen. He had been a youth minister for several years and was still actively involved in ministry to youth. He opened our eyes to the possibility of Youth Ministry as a full time, lifelong professional career. Other visiting youth ministry professors reinforced this relatively new idea through their teaching and life example.

Upon graduation, the Seminary invited me to coordinate the fledgling Youth Ministry program and teach some of its courses. At that point of my life, I had already ministered to youth in the local, district and national settings. My first instinct was to return to local youth ministry full time, but one of my classmates urged me to take on the challenge of heading the Youth Ministry department of our Seminary. Working at the 'grassroots' level, being hands-on with youth was fine, he said, but what an opportunity it would be to train other youth ministers themselves. I saw his wisdom and, since then, I moved on to teach youth pastors in a formal educational setting, mainly at our Seminary.

Having come from the province to study in the city, I had wanted to share what I learned with other places in the Philippines and Asia. I made myself available as a visiting professor to other Bible schools in the provinces. God also opened the way for me to train youth workers in other Asian countries. My network of youth ministers gave me opportunities to mentor the mentors in the city, when I visit the provinces, and even with those in the United States, Canada and the United Kingdom through the internet. Outside the four walls of a school setting, I train youth leaders at camps and retreats.

Besides teaching, writing is my passion. I found my niche when I started writing curriculum for youth, perhaps because it was a great way to combine my two loves: teaching AND writing. Although I have written several articles for magazines and devotional books, I find curriculum writing enjoyable and have written and edited youth lessons that have been published.

Despite my teaching job at the Seminary and Bible schools, speaking at youth camps and writing curricula, I am still involved with my local church's youth group as its consultant and discipler. I serve on a couple of national youth organization boards, and as an advisor to our denomination's national youth organization.

Lorna from Scotland

Staying in one place for a long time can be very difficult. Your stories get old and worn out, your games get tired and well tested, and your energy levels get challenged and defeated on a regular basis. However, the positives outweigh the negatives as you get to see young men and women step into their calling. You see them start to fulfil the potential that is in them and their growth in maturity in Christ. You are blessed by relationships that are deep and meaningful and friendships that will last for ever and into eternity.

But all things must come to an end!

When you do a job that is a calling it is important to not only recognise that calling but recognise when it is complete. If you work in a regular job and keep doing an OK job year after year it is fine to stay there, receive the salary and go through the motions. But in vocational ministry when a congregation is paying your salary an 'OK' job is not good enough. Your heart, passion and calling need to be 100%. When that changes and you find your heart, passion and calling are being directed elsewhere, you need to be honest and step away from the role and the young people that you have spent years investing in. It isn't easy but it is right. Succession planning is important. If you are working well you will be able to step away without destroying what you have built up. You also need to recognise that whoever takes over will do it differently than you did, and that is OK.

I believe that leaving well is as important as the many years that you have put in before you leave. I plan to end my youth ministry leadership role this year. I feel that it is the time to go. How do I know this? Well, for the last three years I have been having a chat with God my Father asking if this is still the job for me. Until this year the answer was always 'You are not quite finished yet'. However, when asking the same question again this past summer I felt very strongly that the answer was different; it was time to 'hang up my boots', i.e. to come off the field of play. I want this final year in my role as St John's youth worker to not just be an OK year but to be a great year. My plan is to take a sabbatical from church for three months to allow the new youth worker space and time to settle into the role without feeling threatened or under scrutiny from me.

I don't plan on leaving my church, however. God may have other ideas and this book will possibly be published before I know what my next role will be. I know that whatever it is it will be exciting, challenging and rewarding. It has been a real privilege to serve as a youth worker and to see many young people turn into amazing young men and women of faith and character who are serving and leading others.

Gary from the USA

Bill was my model and hero who served in youth ministry well into his seventies - a great example for me to emulate. One day near my fiftieth birthday, our newly hired executive pastor asked if I would be willing to provide leadership to adults in the same way I had provided it to students at our church. Since I had served in some areas of wider ministry with parents of teens, particularly fathers, I believed this might be a natural transition to developing a stronger family ministry at our church. This transition had the potential to impact our young people long term if their parents, especially their fathers, led them spiritually at home. It was an interesting season for me as I thought I had been doing my best youth ministry in my forties. I felt confident in leadership development, effective planning, church integration and growing more committed disciples as students graduated to college, to the military or to the workplace.

I believe the decision to move from student ministries into adult ministries was as much an economic decision as an age decision, as the leadership wanted to compensate for the years I had faithfully served our church. The concept of paying me, the youth pastor, the same salary as adult pastors was difficult for the church leadership to justify. The dilemma of properly paying a seasoned youth pastor is a sad reality for most churches and denominations.

My optimistic nature led me to rationalize that this change would allow me to be a stronger advocate for youth ministry, not only in our church but culturally as well. This has become a reality as I have been able to influence our elders and staff to adequately invest in quality youth ministry staff. Overall, this investment is well worth the funds allotted because it ensures a healthy and dynamic church based student ministry.

During a period of pastoral and leadership conflict, I was able to provide direction as an interim lead pastor. The elders and church members were appreciative of the skills I exemplified as I managed so many roles in a calm and confident manner. I contribute this success to my youth ministry experience as I had been challenged with many different roles over my years as the youth pastor. The temporary lead pastor role was not much different than the role of lead youth pastor; it just involved an older population of our church family.

I would strongly suggest that a seasoned youth pastor has some very marketable attributes to be further utilized in the church or even in secular society. Youth ministry develops a variety of skills relationally, technologically, administratively, intergenerationally, in counseling and diplomacy, while working with many different age and interest groups. If someone has been effective in youth ministry for any length of time, their call to serve Jesus and others has been tested, refined and solidified. If that youth pastor applied for a ministry position that matched their spiritual gifts, abilities and passion, they would easily become finalists if I were a member of any pastoral or ministry search team.

For brief videos introducing each of the contributors please go to the website www.firsthalfleadership.com.

QUESTIONS FOR DISCUSSION
OR REFLECTION

Below are the sections each youth pastor covered, followed by some questions for group discussion or reflection.

I. FOUNDATIONS

1. My background and how I got into youth ministry

i. How did you specifically sense a call – or how do you think God is calling you - to work with young people?

ii. Which contributor's call to work with young people do you *most* relate to?

iii. How do young people tend to be viewed/treated in your country, by the church in general, and by *your* church?

2. Looking after your own soul

i. Did anything surprise you about what the writers shared?

ii. As well as the Bible and prayer, what practices tend to help *you* grow spiritually?

iii. Whether you are a volunteer or paid youth worker, what *specifically* do you need to do to protect these practices?

3. Singleness, marriage & children

i. Whose story did you find the most helpful?

ii. What is the *one* thing that sticks in your mind about marriage or singleness as a result of reading all the sections on this subject?

iii. What is the *one* thing you have learned about bringing up children as a result of reading the same sections?

4. Organising yourself and your ministry

i. On a scale of 1 to 10 (with 10 being 'super organised') where would you place yourself?

ii. If you knew a church youth worker or youth pastor when you were a young person, where would you place *them* on the scale? Does this affect your own youth ministry?

iii. Despite their different cultures, is there a consistent theme among all the contributors that you need to take on board and implement?

II. YOUNG PEOPLE

5. Keeping your evangelism edge sharp

i. It is clear from the authors that, as with all areas of youth work, we are stronger in some areas than others. Is evangelism more a strength or weakness for you personally? Is this reflected in your youth ministry?

ii. From what you have read, regardless of culture and language, is there a common factor for success in evangelism in youth ministry?

iii. What do you need to do to encourage evangelism in your work with young people?

6. Communicating with youth

i. How do you tend to prefer communicating with young people: one-to-one, small groups, or from a platform?

ii. Was there any one thing that the authors said that challenges you to communicate more effectively?

iii. In which area(s) do you need to grow to make sure young people are taught and discipled well? For example, building relationships; better understanding of the Bible; planning communication better?

7. Pastoral care of young people

i. How has your own experience of receiving pastoral care as a young person influenced how you deliver pastoral care?

ii. Do you think you should change or adapt the way in which your current youth ministry handles pastoral care?

iii. Who gives *you* pastoral care?

III. OTHER PEOPLE

8. Working with schools

i. The writers' situations are incredibly varied. What is access to schools like in your neighbourhood or country?

ii. What *specific* skills do you bring that the school might be able to use?

iii. Is there an individual at a local school who would be a good person to approach with an offer of help?

9. Leading a team and developing others

i. What factors in your current church make it harder or easier to build and keep a good team of volunteers?

ii. Starting with nothing, how would you go about recruiting a volunteer team of <u>four</u> people to help you lead youth work in a church?

iii. Which piece of advice in the book was most helpful to you?

10. Parents

i. What stood out most from what the authors wrote on this topic?

ii. How does that relate to your experience so far of youth work and working with parents?

iii. What is it that you may now do differently as a result of what you have read?

11. You and senior church leaders

i. Whether it is with the lead/senior pastor or someone else, what is your relationship with your supervisor like?

ii. Does your youth ministry fit in with the overall vision of your church?

iii. Is there anything you need to do, or anyone you need to forgive, to make the relationship between the youth ministry and the wider church ministry better?

IV. OTHER MATTERS

12. Some advice when looking at a new youth ministry role

i. The writers all gave very specific advice. What single piece of advice stands out for you?

ii. If you are serving in a youth ministry role now, what advice would *you* give to someone else applying for a new youth ministry role?

iii. What advice would you give them if they were applying for *your* current youth ministry role?

13. If you are thinking of leaving front line youth ministry

i. What events have taken place to make you think that perhaps your time doing hands-on youth work is coming to an end?

ii. Which author's experience do you most relate to?

iii. What steps do you need to take in order to discern God's will as you consider leaving youth work?

LEADERSHIP DEVELOPMENT
WITH THE ONE WHO BEAT GOLIATH
OUT LATE 2016

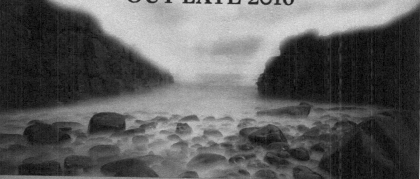

HOW LEADERSHIP TESTS IN YOUR FIRST HALF PREPARE YOU FOR YOUR SECOND

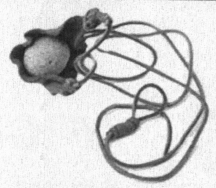

FRASER KEAY

PART OF THE *FIRST HALF LEADERSHIP* SERIES

CPSIA information can be obtained
at www.ICGtesting.com
Printed in the USA
LVHW011825170121
676728LV00007B/1623

9 780995 472907